Scotland Act 1998

CHAPTER 46

Explanatory Notes are available separately

GRANG*IS* UK Publishing

Adapted and published by GRANGIS (Grand Register Library).
Online: www.grangis.com
E-mail: contact@grangis.com

In this version:
ISBN: 979-8-88559-031-0

Note: This is the original version (as it was originally enacted). Title, sub-title and the generated date is as marked on the pages.

Scotland Act 1998

CHAPTER 46

SCOTLAND ACT 1998

PART I

THE SCOTTISH PARLIAMENT

PART V

MISCELLANEOUS AND GENERAL

PART VI

SUPPLEMENTARY

Subordinate legislation

General modification of enactments

Amendments and repeals

Final provisions

SCHEDULES

SCHEDULE 1 — Constituencies, regions and regional members

General

Reports of Boundary Commission

Notices

Reporting and publishing proceedings

4 The standing orders shall include provision for reporting the proceedings...

The Presiding Officer and deputies

5 The standing orders shall include provision for ensuring that the...

Committees

6 (1) Standing orders which provide for the appointment of committees...

Crown interests

7 The standing orders shall include provision for ensuring that a...

SCHEDULE 4 — Enactments etc. protected from modification
Part I — THE PROTECTED PROVISIONS

Particular enactments

1 (1) An Act of the Scottish Parliament cannot modify, or...

The law on reserved matters

2 (1) An Act of the Scottish Parliament cannot modify, or...
3 (1) Paragraph 2 does not apply to modifications which—

This Act

4 (1) An Act of the Scottish Parliament cannot modify, or...

Enactments modified by this Act

5 An Act of the Scottish Parliament cannot modify, or confer...

Shared powers

6 An Act of the Scottish Parliament cannot modify, or confer...
Part II — GENERAL EXCEPTIONS

Restatement, etc.

7 (1) Part I of this Schedule does not prevent an...

Effect of Interpretation Act 1978

8 Part I of this Schedule does not prevent the operation...

Change of title etc.

9 (1) Part I of this Schedule does not prevent an...

Accounts and audit and maladministration

10 Part I of this Schedule does not prevent an Act...

European Communities Act 1972 (c. 68)

15 (1) The European Communities Act 1972 is amended as follows....

Interpretation Act 1978 (c. 30)

16 (1) The Interpretation Act 1978 is amended as follows.

Education (Scotland) Act 1980 (c. 44)

17 In section 135(1) of the Education (Scotland) Act 1980 (interpretation),...

Civil Jurisdiction and Judgments Act 1982 (c. 27)

18 (1) Section 46 of the Civil Jurisdiction and Judgments Act...

Mental Health Act 1983 (c. 20)

19 In section 141 of the Mental Health Act 1983 (members...

National Audit Act 1983 (c. 44)

20 Sections 6 and 7 of the National Audit Act 1983...

Tourism (Overseas Promotion) (Scotland) Act 1984 (c. 4)

21 In section 1 of the Tourism (Overseas Promotion) (Scotland) Act...

Bankruptcy (Scotland) Act 1985 (c. 66)

22 For section 1 of the Bankruptcy (Scotland) Act 1985 there...

Insolvency Act 1986 (c. 45)

23 (1) The Insolvency Act 1986 is amended as follows.

Public Order Act 1986 (c. 64)

24 In section 26(1) of the Public Order Act 1986 (savings...

Copyright, Designs and Patents Act 1988 (c. 48)

25 (1) The Copyright, Designs and Patents Act 1988 is amended...

Official Secrets Act 1989 (c. 6)

26 (1) Section 12 of the Official Secrets Act 1989 (meaning...

Prisons (Scotland) Act 1989 (c. 45)

27 (1) The Prisons (Scotland) Act 1989 is amended as follows....

European Communities (Amendment) Act 1993 (c. 32)

28 In section 6 of the European Communities (Amendment) Act 1993...

Scottish Land Court Act 1993 (c. 45)

29 In section 1 of the Scottish Land Court Act 1993...

Value Added Tax Act 1994 (c. 23)

30 In section 41 of the Value Added Tax Act 1994...

Requirements of Writing (Scotland) Act 1995 (c. 7)

31 In section 12(1) of the Requirements of Writing (Scotland) Act...

Criminal Procedure (Scotland) Act 1995 (c. 46)

32 (1) The Criminal Procedure (Scotland) Act 1995 is amended as...

Defamation Act 1996 (c. 31)

33 (1) The Defamation Act 1996 is amended as follows.

Damages Act 1996 (c. 48)

34 In section 6 of the Damages Act 1996 (guarantees for...

SCHEDULE 9 — Repeals

Scotland Act 1998

1998 CHAPTER 46

An Act to provide for the establishment of a Scottish Parliament and Administration and other changes in the government of Scotland; to provide for changes in the constitution and functions of certain public authorities; to provide for the variation of the basic rate of income tax in relation to income of Scottish taxpayers in accordance with a resolution of the Scottish Parliament; to amend the law about parliamentary constituencies in Scotland; and for connected purposes. [19th November 1998]

Be it enacted by the Queen's most Excellent Majesty, by and with the advice and consent of the Lords Spiritual and Temporal, and Commons, in this present Parliament assembled, and by the authority of the same, as follows:—

PART I

THE SCOTTISH PARLIAMENT

The Scottish Parliament

1 The Scottish Parliament

(1) There shall be a Scottish Parliament.

(2) One member of the Parliament shall be returned for each constituency (under the simple majority system) at an election held in the constituency.

(3) Members of the Parliament for each region shall be returned at a general election under the additional member system of proportional representation provided for in this Part and vacancies among such members shall be filled in accordance with this Part.

(4) The validity of any proceedings of the Parliament is not affected by any vacancy in its membership.

(5) Schedule 1 (which makes provision for the constituencies and regions for the purposes of this Act and the number of regional members) shall have effect.

General elections

2 Ordinary general elections

(1) The day on which the poll at the first ordinary general election for membership of the Parliament shall be held, and the day, time and place for the meeting of the Parliament following that poll, shall be appointed by order made by the Secretary of State.

(2) The poll at subsequent ordinary general elections shall be held on the first Thursday in May in the fourth calendar year following that in which the previous ordinary general election was held, unless the day of the poll is determined by a proclamation under subsection (5).

(3) If the poll is to be held on the first Thursday in May, the Parliament—

(a) is dissolved by virtue of this section at the beginning of the minimum period which ends with that day, and

(b) shall meet within the period of seven days beginning immediately after the day of the poll.

(4) In subsection (3), "the minimum period" means the period determined in accordance with an order under section 12(1).

(5) If the Presiding Officer proposes a day for the holding of the poll which is not more than one month earlier, nor more than one month later, than the first Thursday in May, Her Majesty may by proclamation under the Scottish Seal—

(a) dissolve the Parliament,

(b) require the poll at the election to be held on the day proposed, and

(c) require the Parliament to meet within the period of seven days beginning immediately after the day of the poll.

(6) In this Act "the Scottish Seal" means Her Majesty's Seal appointed by the Treaty of Union to be kept and used in Scotland in place of the Great Seal of Scotland.

3 Extraordinary general elections

(1) The Presiding Officer shall propose a day for the holding of a poll if—

(a) the Parliament resolves that it should be dissolved and, if the resolution is passed on a division, the number of members voting in favour of it is not less than two-thirds of the total number of seats for members of the Parliament, or

(b) any period during which the Parliament is required under section 46 to nominate one of its members for appointment as First Minister ends without such a nomination being made.

(2) If the Presiding Officer makes such a proposal, Her Majesty may by proclamation under the Scottish Seal—

(a) dissolve the Parliament and require an extraordinary general election to be held,

(b) require the poll at the election to be held on the day proposed, and

(c) require the Parliament to meet within the period of seven days beginning immediately after the day of the poll.

(3) If a poll is held under this section within the period of six months ending with the day on which the poll at the next ordinary general election would be held (disregarding section 2(5)), that ordinary general election shall not be held.

(4) Subsection (3) does not affect the year in which the subsequent ordinary general election is to be held.

4 Calculating time for meeting of the Parliament

In calculating any period of days for the purposes of section 2(3)(b) or (5)(c) or section 3(2)(c), Saturday, Sunday, Christmas Eve, Christmas Day, Good Friday, a bank holiday in Scotland or a day appointed for public thanksgiving or mourning shall be disregarded.

5 Candidates

(1) At a general election, the candidates may stand for return as constituency members or regional members.

(2) A person may not be a candidate to be a constituency member for more than one constituency.

(3) The candidates to be regional members shall be those included in a list submitted under subsection (4) or individual candidates.

(4) Any registered political party may submit to the regional returning officer a list of candidates to be regional members for a particular region (referred to in this Act, in relation to the region, as the party's "regional list").

(5) A registered political party's regional list has effect in relation to the general election and any vacancy occurring among the regional members after that election and before the next general election.

(6) Not more than twelve persons may be included in the list (but the list may include only one person).

(7) A registered political party's regional list must not include a person—

- (a) who is included in any other list submitted under subsection (4) for the region or any list submitted under that subsection for another region,
- (b) who is an individual candidate to be a regional member for the region or another region,
- (c) who is a candidate to be a constituency member for a constituency not included in the region, or
- (d) who is a candidate to be a constituency member for a constituency included in the region but is not a candidate of that party.

(8) A person may not be an individual candidate to be a regional member for a particular region if he is—

- (a) included in a list submitted under subsection (4) for the region or another region,
- (b) an individual candidate to be a regional member for another region,

(c) a candidate to be a constituency member for a constituency not included in the region, or

(d) a candidate of any registered political party to be a constituency member for a constituency included in the region.

(9) In this Act, "registered political party" means a party registered under the Registration of Political Parties Act 1998.

6 Poll for regional members

(1) This section and sections 7 and 8 are about the return of regional members at a general election.

(2) In each of the constituencies for the Parliament, a poll shall be held at which each person entitled to vote as elector may give a vote (referred to in this Act as a "regional vote") for—

(a) a registered political party which has submitted a regional list, or

(b) an individual candidate to be a regional member for the region.

(3) The right conferred on a person by subsection (2) is in addition to any right the person may have to vote in any poll for the return of a constituency member.

7 Calculation of regional figures

(1) The persons who are to be returned as constituency members for constituencies included in the region must be determined before the persons who are to be returned as the regional members for the region.

(2) For each registered political party which has submitted a regional list, the regional figure for the purposes of section 8 is—

(a) the total number of regional votes given for the party in all the constituencies included in the region,

divided by

(b) the aggregate of one plus the number of candidates of the party returned as constituency members for any of those constituencies.

(3) Each time a seat is allocated to the party under section 8, that figure shall be recalculated by increasing (or further increasing) the aggregate in subsection (2)(b) by one.

(4) For each individual candidate to be a regional member for the region, the regional figure for the purposes of section 8 is the total number of regional votes given for him in all the constituencies included in the region.

8 Allocation of seats to regional members

(1) The first regional member seat shall be allocated to the registered political party or individual candidate with the highest regional figure.

(2) The second and subsequent regional member seats shall be allocated to the registered political party or individual candidate with the highest regional figure, after any recalculation required by section 7(3) has been carried out.

(3) An individual candidate already returned as a constituency or regional member shall be disregarded.

(4) Seats for the region which are allocated to a registered political party shall be filled by the persons in the party's regional list in the order in which they appear in the list.

(5) For the purposes of this section and section 10, a person in a registered political party's regional list who is returned as a member of the Parliament shall be treated as ceasing to be in the list (even if his return is void).

(6) Once a party's regional list has been exhausted (by the return of persons included in it as constituency members or by the previous application of subsection (1) or (2)) the party shall be disregarded.

(7) If (on the application of subsection (1) or any application of subsection (2)) the highest regional figure is the regional figure of two or more parties or individual candidates, the subsection shall apply to each of them.

Vacancies

9 Constituency vacancies

(1) Where the seat of a constituency member is vacant, an election shall be held to fill the vacancy (subject to subsection (4)).

(2) The date of the poll shall be fixed by the Presiding Officer.

(3) The date shall fall within the period of three months—

(a) beginning with the occurrence of the vacancy, or

(b) if the vacancy does not come to the notice of the Presiding Officer within the period of one month beginning with its occurrence, beginning when it does come to his notice.

(4) The election shall not be held if the latest date for holding the poll would fall within the period of three months ending with the day on which the poll at the next ordinary general election would be held (disregarding section 2(5)).

(5) For the purposes of this section, the date on which a vacancy is to be treated as occurring shall be determined under standing orders.

(6) A person may not be a candidate at such an election if he is a member of the Parliament or a candidate in another election to fill a vacancy.

10 Regional vacancies

(1) This section applies where the seat of a regional member is vacant.

(2) If the regional member was returned as an individual candidate, or the vacancy is not filled in accordance with the following provisions, the seat shall remain vacant until the next general election.

(3) If the regional member was returned (under section 8 or this section) from a registered political party's regional list, the regional returning officer shall notify the Presiding Officer of the name of the person who is to fill the vacancy.

(4) He must be a person who—

(a) is included in that list, and

(b) is willing to serve as a regional member for the region.

(5) Where more than one person satisfies the conditions in subsection (4), the regional returning officer shall notify the name of whichever of them was higher, or highest, in the list.

(6) Where a person's name has been notified under subsection (3), this Act shall apply as if he had been declared to be returned as a regional member for the region on the day on which notification of his name was received by the Presiding Officer.

(7) For the purposes of this section, the date on which a vacancy is to be treated as occurring shall be determined under standing orders.

Franchise and conduct of elections

11 Electors

(1) The persons entitled to vote as electors at an election for membership of the Parliament held in any constituency are those who on the day of the poll—

(a) would be entitled to vote as electors at a local government election in an electoral area falling wholly or partly within the constituency, and

(b) are registered in the register of local government electors at an address within the constituency.

(2) A person is not entitled to vote as elector in any constituency—

(a) more than once at a poll for the return of a constituency member, or

(b) more than once at a poll for the return of regional members,

or to vote as elector in more than one constituency at a general election.

12 Power to make provision about elections

(1) The Secretary of State may by order make provision as to—

(a) the conduct of elections for membership of the Parliament,

(b) the questioning of such an election and the consequences of irregularities, and

(c) the return of members of the Parliament otherwise than at an election.

(2) The provision that may be made under subsection (1)(a) includes, in particular, provision—

(a) about the registration of electors,

(b) for disregarding alterations in a register of electors,

(c) about the limitation of the election expenses of candidates and registered political parties,

(d) for the combination of polls at elections for membership of the Parliament with polls at other elections,

(e) for modifying the application of section 7(1) where the poll at an election for the return of a constituency member is abandoned (or notice of it is countermanded), and

(f) for modifying section 8(7) to ensure the allocation of the correct number of seats for the region.

(3) The provision that may be made under subsection (1)(c) includes, in particular, provision modifying section 10(4) and (5).

(4) An order under subsection (1) may—

(a) apply, with or without modifications or exceptions, any provision made by or under the Representation of the People Acts or the European Parliamentary Elections Act 1978 or by any other enactment relating to parliamentary elections, European Parliamentary elections or local government elections,

(b) modify any form contained in, or in regulations or rules made under, the Representation of the People Acts so far as may be necessary to enable it to be used both for the original purpose and in relation to elections for membership of the Parliament, and

(c) so far as may be necessary in consequence of any provision made by this Act or an order under subsection (1), modify any provision made by any enactment relating to the registration of parliamentary electors or local government electors.

(5) The return of a member of the Parliament at an election may be questioned only under Part III of the Representation of the People Act 1983 as applied by an order under subsection (1).

(6) For the purposes of this Act, the regional returning officer for any region is the person designated as such in accordance with an order made by the Secretary of State under this subsection.

Duration of membership

13 Term of office of members

The term of office of a member of the Parliament begins on the day on which the member is declared to be returned and ends with the dissolution of the Parliament.

14 Resignation of members

A member of the Parliament may at any time resign his seat by giving notice in writing to the Presiding Officer.

Disqualification

15 Disqualification from membership of the Parliament

(1) A person is disqualified from being a member of the Parliament (subject to section 16) if—

(a) he is disqualified from being a member of the House of Commons under paragraphs (a) to (e) of section 1(1) of the House of Commons Disqualification Act 1975 (judges, civil servants, members of the armed forces, members of police forces and members of foreign legislatures),

(b) he is disqualified otherwise than under that Act (either generally or in relation to a particular parliamentary constituency) from being a member of the House of Commons or from sitting and voting in it,

(c) he is a Lord of Appeal in Ordinary, or

(d) he is an office-holder of a description specified in an Order in Council made by Her Majesty under this subsection.

(2) An office-holder of a description specified in an Order in Council made by Her Majesty under this subsection is disqualified from being a member of the Parliament for any constituency or region of a description specified in the Order in relation to the office-holder.

(3) In this section "office-holder" includes employee or other post-holder.

16 Exceptions and relief from disqualification

(1) A person is not disqualified from being a member of the Parliament merely because—

(a) he is a peer (whether of the United Kingdom, Great Britain, England or Scotland), or

(b) he has been ordained or is a minister of any religious denomination.

(2) A citizen of the European Union who is resident in the United Kingdom is not disqualified from being a member of the Parliament merely because of section 3 of the Act of Settlement (disqualification of persons born outside the United Kingdom other than Commonwealth citizens and citizens of the Republic of Ireland).

(3) Subsection (4) applies where a person was, or is alleged to have been, disqualified from being a member of the Parliament (either generally or in relation to a particular constituency or region) on any ground other than one falling within section 15(1)(b).

(4) The Parliament may resolve to disregard any disqualification incurred by that person on the ground in question if it considers that—

(a) the ground has been removed, and

(b) it is proper to disregard any disqualification so incurred.

(5) A resolution under this section shall not—

(a) affect any proceedings under Part III of the Representation of the People Act 1983 as applied by an order under section 12, or

(b) enable the Parliament to disregard any disqualification which has been established in such proceedings or in proceedings under section 18.

17 Effect of disqualification

(1) If a person who is disqualified from being a member of the Parliament or from being a member for a particular constituency or region is returned as a member of the Parliament or (as the case may be) as a member for the constituency or region, his return shall be void and his seat vacant.

(2) If a member of the Parliament becomes disqualified from being a member of the Parliament or from being a member for the particular constituency or region for which he is sitting, he shall cease to be a member of the Parliament (so that his seat is vacant).

(3) Subsections (1) and (2) have effect subject to any resolution of the Parliament under section 16.

(4) Subsection (2) also has effect subject to section 141 of the Mental Health Act 1983 (mental illness) and section 427 of the Insolvency Act 1986 (sequestration etc); and where, in consequence of either of those sections, the seat of a disqualified member of the Parliament is not vacant he shall not cease to be a member of the Parliament until his seat becomes vacant but—

(a) he shall not participate in any proceedings of the Parliament, and

(b) any of his other rights and privileges as a member of the Parliament may be withdrawn by a resolution of the Parliament.

(5) The validity of any proceedings of the Parliament is not affected by the disqualification of any person from being a member of the Parliament or from being a member for the constituency or region for which he purports to sit.

18 Judicial proceedings as to disqualification

(1) Any person who claims that a person purporting to be a member of the Parliament is disqualified or has been disqualified at any time since being returned may apply to the Court of Session for a declarator to that effect.

(2) An application in respect of any person may be made whether the grounds on which it is made are alleged to have subsisted when the person was returned or to have arisen subsequently.

(3) No declarator shall be made—

(a) on grounds which subsisted when the person was returned, if an election petition is pending or has been tried in which the disqualification on those grounds of the person concerned is or was in issue, or

(b) on any ground, if a resolution under section 16 requires that any disqualification incurred on that ground by the person concerned is to be disregarded.

(4) The person in respect of whom an application is made shall be the defender.

(5) The applicant shall give such caution for the expenses of the proceedings as the Court of Session may direct; but any such caution shall not exceed £5,000 or such other sum as the Scottish Ministers may by order specify.

(6) The decision of the court on an application under this section shall be final.

(7) In this section “disqualified” means disqualified from being a member of the Parliament or from being a member for the constituency or region for which the person concerned purports to sit.

Presiding Officer and administration

19 Presiding Officer

(1) The Parliament shall, at its first meeting following a general election, elect from among its members a Presiding Officer and two deputies.

(2) A person elected Presiding Officer or deputy shall hold office until the conclusion of the next election for Presiding Officer under subsection (1) unless he previously

resigns, ceases to be a member of the Parliament otherwise than by virtue of a dissolution or is removed from office by resolution of the Parliament.

(3) If the Presiding Officer or a deputy ceases to hold office before the Parliament is dissolved, the Parliament shall elect another from among its members to fill his place.

(4) The Presiding Officer's functions may be exercised by a deputy if the office of Presiding Officer is vacant or the Presiding Officer is for any reason unable to act.

(5) The Presiding Officer may (subject to standing orders) authorise any deputy to exercise functions on his behalf.

(6) Standing orders may include provision as to the participation (including voting) of the Presiding Officer and deputies in the proceedings of the Parliament.

(7) The validity of any act of the Presiding Officer or a deputy is not affected by any defect in his election.

20 Clerk of the Parliament

(1) There shall be a Clerk of the Parliament.

(2) The Clerk shall be appointed by the Scottish Parliamentary Corporate Body (established under section 21).

(3) The Clerk's functions may be exercised by any Assistant Clerk if the office of Clerk is vacant or the Clerk is for any reason unable to act.

(4) The Clerk may authorise any Assistant Clerk or other member of the staff of the Parliament to exercise functions on his behalf.

21 Scottish Parliamentary Corporate Body

(1) There shall be a body corporate to be known as "The Scottish Parliamentary Corporate Body" (referred to in this Act as the Parliamentary corporation) to perform the functions conferred on the corporation by virtue of this Act or any other enactment.

(2) The members of the corporation shall be—
- (a) the Presiding Officer, and
- (b) four members of the Parliament appointed in accordance with standing orders.

(3) The corporation shall provide the Parliament, or ensure that the Parliament is provided, with the property, staff and services required for the Parliament's purposes.

(4) The Parliament may give special or general directions to the corporation for the purpose of or in connection with the exercise of the corporation's functions.

(5) Any property or liabilities acquired or incurred in relation to matters within the general responsibility of the corporation to which (apart from this subsection) the Parliament would be entitled or subject shall be treated for all purposes as property or (as the case may be) liabilities of the corporation.

(6) Any expenses of the corporation shall be payable out of the Scottish Consolidated Fund.

(7) Any sums received by the corporation shall be paid into that Fund, subject to any provision made by or under an Act of the Scottish Parliament for the disposal of or accounting for such sums.

(8) Schedule 2 (which makes further provision about the corporation) shall have effect.

Proceedings etc.

22 Standing orders

(1) The proceedings of the Parliament shall be regulated by standing orders.

(2) Schedule 3 (which makes provision as to how certain matters are to be dealt with by standing orders) shall have effect.

23 Power to call for witnesses and documents

(1) The Parliament may require any person—

(a) to attend its proceedings for the purpose of giving evidence, or

(b) to produce documents in his custody or under his control,

concerning any subject for which any member of the Scottish Executive has general responsibility.

(2) Subject to subsection (3), the Parliament may impose such a requirement on a person outside Scotland only in connection with the discharge by him of—

(a) functions of the Scottish Administration, or

(b) functions of a Scottish public authority or cross-border public authority, or Border rivers functions (within the meaning of section 111(4)), which concern a subject for which any member of the Scottish Executive has general responsibility.

(3) In relation to the exercise of functions of a Minister of the Crown, the Parliament may not impose such a requirement on—

(a) him (whether or not he continues to be a Minister of the Crown), or

(b) a person who is or has been in Crown employment, within the meaning of section 191(3) of the Employment Rights Act 1996,

unless the exercise concerns a subject for which any member of the Scottish Executive has general responsibility.

(4) But the Parliament may not impose such a requirement in pursuance of subsection (3) in connection with the exercise of functions which are exercisable—

(a) by the Scottish Ministers as well as by a Minister of the Crown, or

(b) by a Minister of the Crown only with the agreement of, or after consultation with, the Scottish Ministers.

(5) Subsection (4)(b) does not prevent the Parliament imposing such a requirement in connection with the exercise of functions which do not relate to reserved matters.

(6) Where all the functions of a body relate to reserved matters, the Parliament may not impose such a requirement on any person in connection with the discharge by him of those functions.

(7) The Parliament may not impose such a requirement on—

(a) a judge of any court, or

(b) a member of any tribunal in connection with the discharge by him of his functions as such.

(8) Such a requirement may be imposed by a committee or sub-committee of the Parliament only if the committee or sub-committee is expressly authorised to do so (whether by standing orders or otherwise).

(9) A person is not obliged under this section to answer any question or produce any document which he would be entitled to refuse to answer or produce in proceedings in a court in Scotland.

(10) A procurator fiscal is not obliged under this section to answer any question or produce any document concerning the operation of the system of criminal prosecution in any particular case if the Lord Advocate—

(a) considers that answering the question or producing the document might prejudice criminal proceedings in that case or would otherwise be contrary to the public interest, and

(b) has authorised the procurator fiscal to decline to answer the question or produce the document on that ground.

24 Witnesses and documents: notice

(1) A requirement under section 23 shall be imposed by the Clerk giving the person in question notice in writing specifying—

(a) the time and place at which the person is to attend and the particular subjects concerning which he is required to give evidence, or

(b) the documents, or types of documents, which he is to produce, the date by which he is to produce them and the particular subjects concerning which they are required.

(2) Such notice shall be given—

(a) in the case of an individual, by sending it, by registered post or the recorded delivery service, addressed to him at his usual or last known address or, where he has given an address for service, at that address,

(b) in any other case, by sending it, by registered post or the recorded delivery service, addressed to the person at the person's registered or principal office.

25 Witnesses and documents: offences

(1) Any person to whom a notice under section 24(1) has been given who—

(a) refuses or fails to attend proceedings as required by the notice,

(b) refuses or fails, when attending proceedings as required by the notice, to answer any question concerning the subjects specified in the notice,

(c) deliberately alters, suppresses, conceals or destroys any document which he is required to produce by the notice, or

(d) refuses or fails to produce any such document,

is guilty of an offence.

(2) Subsection (1) is subject to sections 23(9) and (10) and 27(3).

(3) It is a defence for a person charged with an offence under subsection (1)(a), (b) or (d) to prove that he had a reasonable excuse for the refusal or failure.

(4) A person guilty of an offence under this section is liable on summary conviction to a fine not exceeding level 5 on the standard scale or to imprisonment for a period not exceeding three months.

(5) Where an offence under this section which has been committed by a body corporate is proved to have been committed with the consent or connivance of, or to be attributable to any neglect on the part of—

(a) a director, manager, secretary or other similar officer of the body corporate, or

(b) any person who was purporting to act in any such capacity,

he, as well as the body corporate, is guilty of that offence and liable to be proceeded against accordingly.

26 Witnesses and documents: general

(1) The Presiding Officer or such other person as may be authorised by standing orders may—

(a) administer an oath to any person giving evidence in proceedings of the Parliament, and

(b) require him to take the oath.

(2) Any person who refuses to take an oath when required to do so under subsection (1)(b) is guilty of an offence.

(3) Subsection (4) of section 25 applies to an offence under subsection (2) as it applies to an offence under that section.

(4) Standing orders may provide for the payment of allowances and expenses to persons—

(a) attending proceedings of the Parliament to give evidence, or

(b) producing documents which they have been required or requested to produce,

whether or not in pursuance of a notice under section 24(1).

(5) For the purposes of sections 23 to 25 and this section, a person shall be taken to comply with a requirement to produce a document if he produces a copy of, or an extract of the relevant part of, the document.

27 Participation of the Scottish Law Officers

(1) If the Lord Advocate or the Solicitor General for Scotland is not a member of the Parliament—

(a) he may participate in the proceedings of the Parliament to the extent permitted by standing orders, but may not vote, and

(b) standing orders may in other respects provide that they are to apply to him as if he were such a member.

(2) Subsection (1) is without prejudice to section 39.

(3) The Lord Advocate or the Solicitor General for Scotland may, in any proceedings of the Parliament, decline to answer any question or produce any document relating to the operation of the system of criminal prosecution in any particular case if he considers that answering the question or producing the document—

(a) might prejudice criminal proceedings in that case, or
(b) would otherwise be contrary to the public interest.

Legislation

28 Acts of the Scottish Parliament

(1) Subject to section 29, the Parliament may make laws, to be known as Acts of the Scottish Parliament.

(2) Proposed Acts of the Scottish Parliament shall be known as Bills; and a Bill shall become an Act of the Scottish Parliament when it has been passed by the Parliament and has received Royal Assent.

(3) A Bill receives Royal Assent at the beginning of the day on which Letters Patent under the Scottish Seal signed with Her Majesty's own hand signifying Her Assent are recorded in the Register of the Great Seal.

(4) The date of Royal Assent shall be written on the Act of the Scottish Parliament by the Clerk, and shall form part of the Act.

(5) The validity of an Act of the Scottish Parliament is not affected by any invalidity in the proceedings of the Parliament leading to its enactment.

(6) Every Act of the Scottish Parliament shall be judicially noticed.

(7) This section does not affect the power of the Parliament of the United Kingdom to make laws for Scotland.

29 Legislative competence

(1) An Act of the Scottish Parliament is not law so far as any provision of the Act is outside the legislative competence of the Parliament.

(2) A provision is outside that competence so far as any of the following paragraphs apply—
(a) it would form part of the law of a country or territory other than Scotland, or confer or remove functions exercisable otherwise than in or as regards Scotland,
(b) it relates to reserved matters,
(c) it is in breach of the restrictions in Schedule 4,
(d) it is incompatible with any of the Convention rights or with Community law,
(e) it would remove the Lord Advocate from his position as head of the systems of criminal prosecution and investigation of deaths in Scotland.

(3) For the purposes of this section, the question whether a provision of an Act of the Scottish Parliament relates to a reserved matter is to be determined, subject to subsection (4), by reference to the purpose of the provision, having regard (among other things) to its effect in all the circumstances.

(4) A provision which—
(a) would otherwise not relate to reserved matters, but

(b) makes modifications of Scots private law, or Scots criminal law, as it applies to reserved matters,

is to be treated as relating to reserved matters unless the purpose of the provision is to make the law in question apply consistently to reserved matters and otherwise.

30 Legislative competence: supplementary

(1) Schedule 5 (which defines reserved matters) shall have effect.

(2) Her Majesty may by Order in Council make any modifications of Schedule 4 or 5 which She considers necessary or expedient.

(3) Her Majesty may by Order in Council specify functions which are to be treated, for such purposes of this Act as may be specified, as being, or as not being, functions which are exercisable in or as regards Scotland.

(4) An Order in Council under this section may also make such modifications of—

(a) any enactment or prerogative instrument (including any enactment comprised in or made under this Act), or

(b) any other instrument or document,

as Her Majesty considers necessary or expedient in connection with other provision made by the Order.

31 Scrutiny of Bills before introduction

(1) A member of the Scottish Executive in charge of a Bill shall, on or before introduction of the Bill in the Parliament, state that in his view the provisions of the Bill would be within the legislative competence of the Parliament.

(2) The Presiding Officer shall, on or before the introduction of a Bill in the Parliament, decide whether or not in his view the provisions of the Bill would be within the legislative competence of the Parliament and state his decision.

(3) The form of any statement, and the manner in which it is to be made, shall be determined under standing orders, and standing orders may provide for any statement to be published.

32 Submission of Bills for Royal Assent

(1) It is for the Presiding Officer to submit Bills for Royal Assent.

(2) The Presiding Officer shall not submit a Bill for Royal Assent at any time when—

(a) the Advocate General, the Lord Advocate or the Attorney General is entitled to make a reference in relation to the Bill under section 33,

(b) any such reference has been made but has not been decided or otherwise disposed of by the Judicial Committee, or

(c) an order may be made in relation to the Bill under section 35.

(3) The Presiding Officer shall not submit a Bill in its unamended form for Royal Assent if—

(a) the Judicial Committee have decided that the Bill or any provision of it would not be within the legislative competence of the Parliament, or

(b) a reference made in relation to the Bill under section 33 has been withdrawn following a request for withdrawal of the reference under section 34(2)(b).

(4) In this Act—

"Advocate General" means the Advocate General for Scotland,

"Judicial Committee" means the Judicial Committee of the Privy Council.

33 Scrutiny of Bills by the Judicial Committee

(1) The Advocate General, the Lord Advocate or the Attorney General may refer the question of whether a Bill or any provision of a Bill would be within the legislative competence of the Parliament to the Judicial Committee for decision.

(2) Subject to subsection (3), he may make a reference in relation to a Bill at any time during—

(a) the period of four weeks beginning with the passing of the Bill, and

(b) any period of four weeks beginning with any subsequent approval of the Bill in accordance with standing orders made by virtue of section 36(5).

(3) He shall not make a reference in relation to a Bill if he has notified the Presiding Officer that he does not intend to make a reference in relation to the Bill, unless the Bill has been approved as mentioned in subsection (2)(b) since the notification.

34 ECJ references

(1) This section applies where—

(a) a reference has been made in relation to a Bill under section 33,

(b) a reference for a preliminary ruling has been made by the Judicial Committee in connection with that reference, and

(c) neither of those references has been decided or otherwise disposed of.

(2) If the Parliament resolves that it wishes to reconsider the Bill—

(a) the Presiding Officer shall notify the Advocate General, the Lord Advocate and the Attorney General of that fact, and

(b) the person who made the reference in relation to the Bill under section 33 shall request the withdrawal of the reference.

(3) In this section "a reference for a preliminary ruling" means a reference of a question to the European Court under Article 177 of the Treaty establishing the European Community, Article 41 of the Treaty establishing the European Coal and Steel Community or Article 150 of the Treaty establishing the European Atomic Energy Community.

35 Power to intervene in certain cases

(1) If a Bill contains provisions—

(a) which the Secretary of State has reasonable grounds to believe would be incompatible with any international obligations or the interests of defence or national security, or

(b) which make modifications of the law as it applies to reserved matters and which the Secretary of State has reasonable grounds to believe would have an adverse effect on the operation of the law as it applies to reserved matters, he may make an order prohibiting the Presiding Officer from submitting the Bill for Royal Assent.

(2) The order must identify the Bill and the provisions in question and state the reasons for making the order.

(3) The order may be made at any time during—

(a) the period of four weeks beginning with the passing of the Bill,

(b) any period of four weeks beginning with any subsequent approval of the Bill in accordance with standing orders made by virtue of section 36(5),

(c) if a reference is made in relation to the Bill under section 33, the period of four weeks beginning with the reference being decided or otherwise disposed of by the Judicial Committee.

(4) The Secretary of State shall not make an order in relation to a Bill if he has notified the Presiding Officer that he does not intend to do so, unless the Bill has been approved as mentioned in subsection (3)(b) since the notification.

(5) An order in force under this section at a time when such approval is given shall cease to have effect.

36 Stages of Bills

(1) Standing orders shall include provision—

(a) for general debate on a Bill with an opportunity for members to vote on its general principles,

(b) for the consideration of, and an opportunity for members to vote on, the details of a Bill, and

(c) for a final stage at which a Bill can be passed or rejected.

(2) Subsection (1) does not prevent standing orders making provision to enable the Parliament to expedite proceedings in relation to a particular Bill.

(3) Standing orders may make provision different from that required by subsection (1) for the procedure applicable to Bills of any of the following kinds—

(a) Bills which restate the law,

(b) Bills which repeal spent enactments,

(c) private Bills.

(4) Standing orders shall provide for an opportunity for the reconsideration of a Bill after its passing if (and only if)—

(a) the Judicial Committee decide that the Bill or any provision of it would not be within the legislative competence of the Parliament,

(b) a reference made in relation to the Bill under section 33 is withdrawn following a request for withdrawal of the reference under section 34(2)(b), or

(c) an order is made in relation to the Bill under section 35.

(5) Standing orders shall, in particular, ensure that any Bill amended on reconsideration is subject to a final stage at which it can be approved or rejected.

(6) References in subsection (4), sections 28(2) and 38(1)(a) and paragraph 7 of Schedule 3 to the passing of a Bill shall, in the case of a Bill which has been amended on reconsideration, be read as references to the approval of the Bill.

Other provisions

37 Acts of Union

The Union with Scotland Act 1706 and the Union with England Act 1707 have effect subject to this Act.

38 Letters Patent and proclamations

(1) The Keeper of the Registers of Scotland shall record in the Register of the Great Seal—

(a) all Letters Patent signed with Her Majesty's own hand signifying Her Assent to a Bill passed by the Parliament, and

(b) all royal proclamations under sections 2(5) and 3(2),

which have passed under the Scottish Seal.

(2) On recording such Letters Patent he shall intimate the date of recording to the Clerk.

(3) Her Majesty may by Order in Council make provision as to—

(a) the form and manner of preparation, and

(b) the publication,

of such Letters Patent and proclamations.

(4) If the First Minister so directs, impressions with the same device as the Scottish Seal shall be taken in such manner, of such size and on such material as is specified in the direction.

(5) Each such impression—

(a) shall be known as a Wafer Scottish Seal, and

(b) shall be kept in accordance with directions of the First Minister.

(6) If a Wafer Scottish Seal has been applied to Letters Patent or a proclamation mentioned in subsection (1), the document has the same validity as if it had passed under the Scottish Seal.

39 Members' interests

(1) Provision shall be made for a register of interests of members of the Parliament and for the register to be published and made available for public inspection.

(2) Provision shall be made—

(a) requiring members of the Parliament to register in that register financial interests (including benefits in kind), as defined for the purposes of this paragraph,

(b) requiring that any member of the Parliament who has a financial interest (including benefits in kind), as defined for the purposes of this paragraph, in any matter declares that interest before taking part in any proceedings of the Parliament relating to that matter.

(3) Provision made in pursuance of subsection (2) shall include any provision which the Parliament considers appropriate for preventing or restricting the participation in proceedings of the Parliament of a member with an interest defined for the purposes of subsection (2)(a) or (b) in a matter to which the proceedings relate.

(4) Provision shall be made prohibiting a member of the Parliament from—

(a) advocating or initiating any cause or matter on behalf of any person, by any means specified in the provision, in consideration of any payment or benefit in kind of a description so specified, or

(b) urging, in consideration of any such payment or benefit in kind, any other member of the Parliament to advocate or initiate any cause or matter on behalf of any person by any such means.

(5) Provision made in pursuance of subsections (2) to (4) shall include any provision which the Parliament considers appropriate for excluding from proceedings of the Parliament any member who fails to comply with, or contravenes, any provision made in pursuance of those subsections.

(6) Any member of the Parliament who—

(a) takes part in any proceedings of the Parliament without having complied with, or in contravention of, any provision made in pursuance of subsection (2) or (3), or

(b) contravenes any provision made in pursuance of subsection (4),

is guilty of an offence.

(7) A person guilty of an offence under subsection (6) is liable on summary conviction to a fine not exceeding level 5 on the standard scale.

(8) In this section—

(a) "provision" means provision made by or under an Act of the Scottish Parliament,

(b) references to members of the Parliament include references to the Lord Advocate and the Solicitor General for Scotland, whether or not they are such members.

Legal issues

40 Proceedings by or against the Parliament etc

(1) Proceedings by or against the Parliament shall be instituted by or (as the case may be) against the Parliamentary corporation on behalf of the Parliament.

(2) Proceedings by or against—

(a) the Presiding Officer or a deputy, or

(b) any member of the staff of the Parliament,

shall be instituted by or (as the case may be) against the corporation on his behalf.

(3) In any proceedings against the Parliament, the court shall not make an order for suspension, interdict, reduction or specific performance (or other like order) but may instead make a declarator.

(4) In any proceedings against—

(a) any member of the Parliament,

(b) the Presiding Officer or a deputy,

(c) any member of the staff of the Parliament, or

(d) the Parliamentary corporation,

the court shall not make an order for suspension, interdict, reduction or specific performance (or other like order) if the effect of doing so would be to give any relief against the Parliament which could not have been given in proceedings against the Parliament.

(5) References in this section to an order include an interim order.

41 Defamatory statements

(1) For the purposes of the law of defamation—

- (a) any statement made in proceedings of the Parliament, and
- (b) the publication under the authority of the Parliament of any statement,

shall be absolutely privileged.

(2) In subsection (1), "statement" has the same meaning as in the Defamation Act 1996.

42 Contempt of court

(1) The strict liability rule shall not apply in relation to any publication—

- (a) made in proceedings of the Parliament in relation to a Bill or subordinate legislation, or
- (b) to the extent that it consists of a fair and accurate report of such proceedings made in good faith.

(2) In subsection (1), "the strict liability rule" and "publication" have the same meanings as in the Contempt of Court Act 1981.

43 Corrupt practices

The Parliament shall be a public body for the purposes of the Prevention of Corruption Acts 1889 to 1916.

PART II

THE SCOTTISH ADMINISTRATION

Ministers and their staff

44 The Scottish Executive

(1) There shall be a Scottish Executive, whose members shall be—

- (a) the First Minister,
- (b) such Ministers as the First Minister may appoint under section 47, and
- (c) the Lord Advocate and the Solicitor General for Scotland.

(2) The members of the Scottish Executive are referred to collectively as the Scottish Ministers.

(3) A person who holds a Ministerial office may not be appointed a member of the Scottish Executive; and if a member of the Scottish Executive is appointed to a Ministerial office he shall cease to hold office as a member of the Scottish Executive.

(4) In subsection (3), references to a member of the Scottish Executive include a junior Scottish Minister and "Ministerial office" has the same meaning as in section 2 of the House of Commons Disqualification Act 1975.

45 The First Minister

(1) The First Minister shall be appointed by Her Majesty from among the members of the Parliament and shall hold office at Her Majesty's pleasure.

(2) The First Minister may at any time tender his resignation to Her Majesty and shall do so if the Parliament resolves that the Scottish Executive no longer enjoys the confidence of the Parliament.

(3) The First Minister shall cease to hold office if a person is appointed in his place.

(4) If the office of First Minister is vacant or he is for any reason unable to act, the functions exercisable by him shall be exercisable by a person designated by the Presiding Officer.

(5) A person shall be so designated only if—

(a) he is a member of the Parliament, or

(b) if the Parliament has been dissolved, he is a person who ceased to be a member by virtue of the dissolution.

(6) Functions exercisable by a person by virtue of subsection (5)(a) shall continue to be exercisable by him even if the Parliament is dissolved.

(7) The First Minister shall be the Keeper of the Scottish Seal.

46 Choice of the First Minister

(1) If one of the following events occurs, the Parliament shall within the period allowed nominate one of its members for appointment as First Minister.

(2) The events are—

(a) the holding of a poll at a general election,

(b) the First Minister tendering his resignation to Her Majesty,

(c) the office of First Minister becoming vacant (otherwise than in consequence of his so tendering his resignation),

(d) the First Minister ceasing to be a member of the Parliament otherwise than by virtue of a dissolution.

(3) The period allowed is the period of 28 days which begins with the day on which the event in question occurs; but—

(a) if another of those events occurs within the period allowed, that period shall be extended (subject to paragraph (b)) so that it ends with the period of 28 days beginning with the day on which that other event occurred, and

(b) the period shall end if the Parliament passes a resolution under section 3(1)(a) or when Her Majesty appoints a person as First Minister.

(4) The Presiding Officer shall recommend to Her Majesty the appointment of any member of the Parliament who is nominated by the Parliament under this section.

47 Ministers

(1) The First Minister may, with the approval of Her Majesty, appoint Ministers from among the members of the Parliament.

(2) The First Minister shall not seek Her Majesty's approval for any appointment under this section without the agreement of the Parliament.

(3) A Minister appointed under this section—

(a) shall hold office at Her Majesty's pleasure,

(b) may be removed from office by the First Minister,

(c) may at any time resign and shall do so if the Parliament resolves that the Scottish Executive no longer enjoys the confidence of the Parliament,

(d) if he resigns, shall cease to hold office immediately, and

(e) shall cease to hold office if he ceases to be a member of the Parliament otherwise than by virtue of a dissolution.

48 The Scottish Law Officers

(1) It is for the First Minister to recommend to Her Majesty the appointment or removal of a person as Lord Advocate or Solicitor General for Scotland; but he shall not do so without the agreement of the Parliament.

(2) The Lord Advocate and the Solicitor General for Scotland may at any time resign and shall do so if the Parliament resolves that the Scottish Executive no longer enjoys the confidence of the Parliament.

(3) Where the Lord Advocate resigns in consequence of such a resolution, he shall be deemed to continue in office until the warrant of appointment of the person succeeding to the office of Lord Advocate is granted, but only for the purpose of exercising his retained functions.

(4) Subsection (3) is without prejudice to section 287 of the Criminal Procedure (Scotland) Act 1995 (demission of office by Lord Advocate).

(5) Any decision of the Lord Advocate in his capacity as head of the systems of criminal prosecution and investigation of deaths in Scotland shall continue to be taken by him independently of any other person.

(6) In Schedule 2 to the House of Commons Disqualification Act 1975 (Ministerial offices) and Part III of Schedule 1 to the Ministerial and other Salaries Act 1975 (salaries of the Law Officers), the entries for the Lord Advocate and the Solicitor General for Scotland are omitted.

49 Junior Scottish Ministers

(1) The First Minister may, with the approval of Her Majesty, appoint persons from among the members of the Parliament to assist the Scottish Ministers in the exercise of their functions.

(2) They shall be known as junior Scottish Ministers.

(3) The First Minister shall not seek Her Majesty's approval for any appointment under this section without the agreement of the Parliament.

(4) A junior Scottish Minister—
(a) shall hold office at Her Majesty's pleasure,
(b) may be removed from office by the First Minister,
(c) may at any time resign and shall do so if the Parliament resolves that the Scottish Executive no longer enjoys the confidence of the Parliament,
(d) if he resigns, shall cease to hold office immediately, and
(e) shall cease to hold office if he ceases to be a member of the Parliament otherwise than by virtue of a dissolution.

50 Validity of acts of Scottish Ministers etc

The validity of any act of a member of the Scottish Executive or junior Scottish Minister is not affected by any defect in his nomination by the Parliament or (as the case may be) in the Parliament's agreement to his appointment.

51 The Civil Service

(1) The Scottish Ministers may appoint persons to be members of the staff of the Scottish Administration.

(2) Service as—
(a) the holder of any office in the Scottish Administration which is not a ministerial office, or
(b) a member of the staff of the Scottish Administration,

shall be service in the Home Civil Service.

(3) Subsection (1) and the other enactments conferring power to appoint such persons shall have effect subject to any provision made in relation to the Home Civil Service by or under any Order in Council.

(4) Any Civil Service management function shall be exercisable by the Minister for the Civil Service in relation to the persons mentioned in subsection (2) as it is exercisable in relation to other members of the Home Civil Service; and, accordingly, section 1 of the Civil Service (Management Functions) Act 1992 (delegation of functions by Ministers) shall apply to any such function as extended by this section.

(5) Any salary or allowances payable to or in respect of the persons mentioned in subsection (2) (including contributions to any pension scheme) shall be payable out of the Scottish Consolidated Fund.

(6) Section 1(2) and (3) of the Superannuation Act 1972 (delegation of functions relating to civil service superannuation schemes etc.) shall have effect as if references to a Minister of the Crown (other than the Minister for the Civil Service) included the Scottish Ministers.

(7) The Scottish Ministers shall make payments to the Minister for the Civil Service, at such times as he may determine, of such amounts as he may determine in respect of—
(a) the provision of pensions, allowances or gratuities by virtue of section 1 of the Superannuation Act 1972 to or in respect of persons who are or have been in such service as is mentioned in subsection (2), and
(b) any expenses to be incurred in administering those pensions, allowances or gratuities.

(8) Amounts required for payments under subsection (7) shall be charged on the Scottish Consolidated Fund.

(9) In this section—

"Civil Service management function" means any function to which section 1 of the Civil Service (Management Functions) Act 1992 applies and which is vested in the Minister for the Civil Service,

"the Home Civil Service" means Her Majesty's Home Civil Service.

Ministerial functions

52 Exercise of functions

(1) Statutory functions may be conferred on the Scottish Ministers by that name.

(2) Statutory functions of the Scottish Ministers, the First Minister or the Lord Advocate shall be exercisable on behalf of Her Majesty.

(3) Statutory functions of the Scottish Ministers shall be exercisable by any member of the Scottish Executive.

(4) Any act or omission of, or in relation to, any member of the Scottish Executive shall be treated as an act or omission of, or in relation to, each of them; and any property acquired, or liability incurred, by any member of the Scottish Executive shall be treated accordingly.

(5) Subsection (4) does not apply in relation to the exercise of—
- (a) functions conferred on the First Minister alone, or
- (b) retained functions of the Lord Advocate.

(6) In this Act, "retained functions" in relation to the Lord Advocate means—
- (a) any functions exercisable by him immediately before he ceases to be a Minister of the Crown, and
- (b) other statutory functions conferred on him alone after he ceases to be a Minister of the Crown.

(7) In this section, "statutory functions" means functions conferred by virtue of any enactment.

53 General transfer of functions

(1) The functions mentioned in subsection (2) shall, so far as they are exercisable within devolved competence, be exercisable by the Scottish Ministers instead of by a Minister of the Crown.

(2) Those functions are—
- (a) those of Her Majesty's prerogative and other executive functions which are exercisable on behalf of Her Majesty by a Minister of the Crown,
- (b) other functions conferred on a Minister of the Crown by a prerogative instrument, and
- (c) functions conferred on a Minister of the Crown by any pre-commencement enactment,

but do not include any retained functions of the Lord Advocate.

(3) In this Act, "pre-commencement enactment" means—

(a) an Act passed before or in the same session as this Act and any other enactment made before the passing of this Act,

(b) an enactment made, before the commencement of this section, under such an Act or such other enactment,

(c) subordinate legislation under section 106, to the extent that the legislation states that it is to be treated as a pre-commencement enactment.

(4) This section and section 54 are modified by Part III of Schedule 4.

54 Devolved competence

(1) References in this Act to the exercise of a function being within or outside devolved competence are to be read in accordance with this section.

(2) It is outside devolved competence—

(a) to make any provision by subordinate legislation which would be outside the legislative competence of the Parliament if it were included in an Act of the Scottish Parliament, or

(b) to confirm or approve any subordinate legislation containing such provision.

(3) In the case of any function other than a function of making, confirming or approving subordinate legislation, it is outside devolved competence to exercise the function (or exercise it in any way) so far as a provision of an Act of the Scottish Parliament conferring the function (or, as the case may be, conferring it so as to be exercisable in that way) would be outside the legislative competence of the Parliament.

55 Functions exercisable with agreement

(1) A statutory provision, or any provision not contained in an enactment, which provides for a Minister of the Crown to exercise a function with the agreement of, or after consultation with, any other Minister of the Crown shall cease to have effect in relation to the exercise of the function by a member of the Scottish Executive by virtue of section 53.

(2) In subsection (1) "statutory provision" means any provision in a pre-commencement enactment other than paragraph 5 or 15 of Schedule 32 to the Local Government, Planning and Land Act 1980 (designation of enterprise zones).

56 Shared powers

(1) Despite the transfer by virtue of section 53 of any function under—

(a) section 17(1) of the Ministry of Transport Act 1919 (power to make advances for certain purposes),

(b) any Order in Council under section 1 of the United Nations Act 1946 (measures to give effect to Security Council decisions),

(c) section 9 of the Industrial Organisation and Development Act 1947 (levies for scientific research, promotion of exports, etc.),

(d) section 5 of the Science and Technology Act 1965 (funding of scientific research),

(e) section 1 of the Mineral Exploration and Investment Grants Act 1972 (contributions in respect of mineral exploration),

(f) sections 10 to 12 of the Industry Act 1972 (credits and grants for construction of ships and offshore installations),

(g) sections 2, 11(3) and 12(4) of the Employment and Training Act 1973 (power to make arrangements for employment and training etc. and to make certain payments),

(h) sections 7 to 9 and 11 to 13 of the Industrial Development Act 1982 (financial and other assistance for industry), and

(i) sections 39 and 40 of the Road Traffic Act 1988 (road safety information and training),

the function shall be exercisable by a Minister of the Crown as well as by the Scottish Ministers.

(2) Despite the transfer of any other function by virtue of section 53, the function shall, if subordinate legislation so provides, be exercisable (or be exercisable so far as the legislation provides) by a Minister of the Crown as well as by the Scottish Ministers.

(3) Subordinate legislation under subsection (2) may not be made so as to come into force at any time after the function in question has become exercisable by the Scottish Ministers.

(4) Any power referred to in section 53(2)(a) to establish, maintain or abolish a body, office or office-holder having functions which include both—

(a) functions which are exercisable in or as regards Scotland and do not relate to reserved matters, and

(b) other functions,

shall, despite that section, be exercisable jointly by the Minister of the Crown and the Scottish Ministers.

(5) In subsection (4), "office-holder" includes employee or other post-holder.

57 Community law and Convention rights

(1) Despite the transfer to the Scottish Ministers by virtue of section 53 of functions in relation to observing and implementing obligations under Community law, any function of a Minister of the Crown in relation to any matter shall continue to be exercisable by him as regards Scotland for the purposes specified in section 2(2) of the European Communities Act 1972.

(2) A member of the Scottish Executive has no power to make any subordinate legislation, or to do any other act, so far as the legislation or act is incompatible with any of the Convention rights or with Community law.

(3) Subsection (2) does not apply to an act of the Lord Advocate—

(a) in prosecuting any offence, or

(b) in his capacity as head of the systems of criminal prosecution and investigation of deaths in Scotland,

which, because of subsection (2) of section 6 of the Human Rights Act 1998, is not unlawful under subsection (1) of that section.

58 Power to prevent or require action

(1) If the Secretary of State has reasonable grounds to believe that any action proposed to be taken by a member of the Scottish Executive would be incompatible with any international obligations, he may by order direct that the proposed action shall not be taken.

(2) If the Secretary of State has reasonable grounds to believe that any action capable of being taken by a member of the Scottish Executive is required for the purpose of giving effect to any such obligations, he may by order direct that the action shall be taken.

(3) In subsections (1) and (2), "action" includes making, confirming or approving subordinate legislation and, in subsection (2), includes introducing a Bill in the Parliament.

(4) If any subordinate legislation made or which could be revoked by a member of the Scottish Executive contains provisions—

(a) which the Secretary of State has reasonable grounds to believe to be incompatible with any international obligations or the interests of defence or national security, or

(b) which make modifications of the law as it applies to reserved matters and which the Secretary of State has reasonable grounds to believe to have an adverse effect on the operation of the law as it applies to reserved matters,

the Secretary of State may by order revoke the legislation.

(5) An order under this section must state the reasons for making the order.

Property and liabilities

59 Property and liabilities of the Scottish Ministers

(1) Property may be held by the Scottish Ministers by that name.

(2) Property acquired by or transferred to the Scottish Ministers shall belong to, and liabilities incurred by the Scottish Ministers shall be liabilities of, the Scottish Ministers for the time being.

(3) In relation to property to be acquired by or transferred to, or belonging to, the Scottish Ministers or liabilities incurred by the Scottish Ministers, references to the Scottish Ministers—

(a) in any title recorded in the Register of Sasines or registered in the Land Register of Scotland, or

(b) in any other document,

shall be read in accordance with subsection (2).

(4) A document shall be validly executed by the Scottish Ministers if it is executed by any member of the Scottish Executive.

60 Transfers to the Scottish Ministers

(1) Subordinate legislation may provide—

(a) for the transfer to the Scottish Ministers of any property belonging to a Minister of the Crown or government department, or

(b) for the Scottish Ministers to have such rights or interests in relation to any property belonging to a Minister of the Crown or government department as the person making the legislation considers appropriate (whether in connection with a transfer or otherwise).

(2) Subordinate legislation may provide for the transfer to the Scottish Ministers of any liabilities to which a Minister of the Crown or government department is subject.

(3) Subordinate legislation under this section may only be made in connection with any transfer or sharing of functions of a Minister of the Crown by virtue of section 53, 63 or 89 or in any other circumstances in which the person making the legislation considers it appropriate to do so for the purposes of this Act.

61 Property and liabilities of the Lord Advocate and the First Minister

(1) Property may be held by the Lord Advocate by that name.

(2) Property acquired by or transferred to the Lord Advocate shall belong to, and liabilities incurred by the Lord Advocate shall be liabilities of, the Lord Advocate for the time being.

(3) In relation to property to be acquired by or transferred to, or belonging to, the Lord Advocate or liabilities incurred by the Lord Advocate, references to the Lord Advocate—

(a) in any title recorded in the Register of Sasines or registered in the Land Register of Scotland, or

(b) in any other document,

shall be read in accordance with subsection (2).

(4) Any rights and liabilities acquired or incurred by the First Minister shall be rights or (as the case may be) liabilities of the First Minister for the time being.

62 Transfers to the Lord Advocate

(1) Subordinate legislation may provide—

(a) for the transfer to the Lord Advocate of any property belonging to a Minister of the Crown or government department, or

(b) for the Lord Advocate to have such rights or interests in relation to any property belonging to a Minister of the Crown or government department as the person making the legislation considers appropriate (whether in connection with a transfer or otherwise).

(2) Subordinate legislation may provide for the transfer to the Lord Advocate of any liabilities to which a Minister of the Crown or government department is subject.

(3) Subordinate legislation under this section may only be made in connection with the Lord Advocate becoming a member of the Scottish Executive or having any retained functions or in any other circumstances in which the person making the legislation considers it appropriate to do so for the purposes of this Act.

Transfer of additional functions

63 Power to transfer functions

(1) Her Majesty may by Order in Council provide for any functions, so far as they are exercisable by a Minister of the Crown in or as regards Scotland, to be exercisable—

(a) by the Scottish Ministers instead of by the Minister of the Crown,

(b) by the Scottish Ministers concurrently with the Minister of the Crown, or

(c) by the Minister of the Crown only with the agreement of, or after consultation with, the Scottish Ministers.

(2) Where an Order is made under subsection (1)(a) or (b) in relation to a function of a Minister of the Crown which is exercisable only with the agreement of, or after consultation with, another Minister of the Crown, the function shall, unless the Order provides otherwise, be exercisable by the Scottish Ministers free from any such requirement.

(3) An Order under this section may, in particular, provide for any function exercisable by the Scottish Ministers by virtue of an Order under subsection (1)(a) or (b) to be exercisable subject to a requirement for the function to be exercised with the agreement of, or after consultation with, a Minister of the Crown or other person.

PART III

FINANCIAL PROVISIONS

64 Scottish Consolidated Fund

(1) There shall be a Scottish Consolidated Fund.

(2) The Secretary of State shall from time to time make payments into the Fund out of money provided by Parliament of such amounts as he may determine.

(3) Sums received by an office-holder in the Scottish Administration shall be paid into the Fund.

(4) Subsection (3) is subject to any provision made by or under an Act of the Scottish Parliament for the disposal of or accounting for such sums.

(5) The Treasury may, after consulting with the Scottish Ministers, by order designate receipts of any description specified in the order which are payable into the Fund (or would be but for any provision made by or under an Act of the Scottish Parliament).

(6) The Scottish Ministers shall make payments to the Secretary of State, at such times and by such methods as the Treasury may from time to time determine, of sums equal to the total amount outstanding in respect of designated receipts.

(7) Amounts required for the payment of sums under subsection (6) shall be charged on the Fund.

(8) The Fund shall be held with the Paymaster General.

65 Payments out of the Fund

(1) A sum may only be paid out of the Scottish Consolidated Fund if—

(a) it has been charged on the Fund by any enactment,

(b) it is payable out of the Fund without further approval by virtue of this Act, or

(c) it is paid out for or in connection with any of the purposes mentioned in subsection (2) in accordance with rules made by or under an Act of the Scottish Parliament.

(2) Those purposes are—

(a) meeting expenditure of the Scottish Administration,

(b) meeting expenditure payable out of the Fund under any enactment.

(3) A sum paid out of the Fund shall not be applied for any purpose other than that for which it was charged or (as the case may be) paid out.

66 Borrowing by the Scottish Ministers etc

(1) The Scottish Ministers may borrow from the Secretary of State any sums required by them for the purpose of—

(a) meeting a temporary excess of sums paid out of the Scottish Consolidated Fund over sums paid into that Fund, or

(b) providing a working balance in the Fund.

(2) Amounts required for the repayment of, or the payment of interest on, sums borrowed under this section shall be charged on the Fund.

(3) Sums borrowed under this section shall be repaid to the Secretary of State at such times and by such methods, and interest on them shall be paid to him at such rates and at such times, as the Treasury may from time to time determine.

(4) A member of the Scottish Executive may borrow money only under this section or under any power conferred by any other Act of Parliament.

67 Lending by the Secretary of State

(1) The Treasury may issue to the Secretary of State out of the National Loans Fund such sums as are required by him for making loans under section 66.

(2) The aggregate at any time outstanding in respect of the principal of sums borrowed under that section shall not exceed £500 million.

(3) The Secretary of State may by order made with the consent of the Treasury substitute for the amount (or substituted amount) specified in subsection (2) such increased amount as may be specified in the order.

(4) Sums received by the Secretary of State under section 66(3) shall be paid into the National Loans Fund.

68 Borrowing by statutory bodies

(1) If a member of the Scottish Executive lends money to a body established under any enactment, the rate of interest on the loan shall not be less than the lowest rate

determined by the Treasury under section 5 of the National Loans Act 1968 in respect of similar loans made out of the National Loans Fund on the day the loan is made.

(2) A body established under any enactment shall not, in pursuance of a power conferred by virtue of an Act of the Scottish Parliament, borrow money in a currency other than sterling except with the consent of the Scottish Ministers given with the approval of the Treasury.

69 The Auditor General for Scotland

(1) There shall be an Auditor General for Scotland who shall be an individual appointed by Her Majesty on the nomination of the Parliament.

(2) A recommendation shall not be made to Her Majesty for the removal from office of the Auditor General for Scotland unless the Parliament so resolves and, if the resolution is passed on a division, the number of members voting in favour is not less than two-thirds of the total number of seats for members of the Parliament.

(3) The validity of any act of the Auditor General for Scotland is not affected by any defect in his nomination by the Parliament.

(4) The Auditor General for Scotland shall not, in the exercise of any of his functions, be subject to the direction or control of any member of the Scottish Executive or of the Parliament.

(5) Subsection (4) does not apply in relation to any function conferred on him of preparing accounts.

70 Financial control, accounts and audit

(1) Scottish legislation shall provide—
- (a) for proper accounts to be prepared by the Scottish Ministers, by the Lord Advocate and by other persons to whom sums are paid out of the Scottish Consolidated Fund, of their expenditure and receipts,
- (b) for the Scottish Ministers to prepare an account of payments into and out of the Fund,
- (c) for the Auditor General for Scotland to exercise, or ensure the exercise by other persons of, the functions mentioned in subsection (2),
- (d) for access by persons exercising those functions to such documents as they may reasonably require,
- (e) for members of the staff of the Scottish Administration designated for the purpose to be answerable to the Parliament in respect of the expenditure and receipts of each part of the Scottish Administration, and
- (f) for the publication of parliamentary accounts and of reports on such accounts and for the laying of such accounts and reports before the Parliament.

(2) The functions referred to in subsection (1)(c) are—
- (a) issuing credits for the payment of sums out of the Fund,
- (b) examining parliamentary accounts (which includes determining whether sums paid out of the Fund have been paid out and applied in accordance with section 65), and certifying and reporting on them,

(c) carrying out examinations into the economy, efficiency and effectiveness with which the Scottish Ministers and the Lord Advocate have used their resources in discharging their functions, and

(d) carrying out examinations into the economy, efficiency and effectiveness with which other persons determined under Scottish legislation to whom sums are paid out of the Fund have used those sums in discharging their functions.

(3) Standing orders shall provide for the consideration by the Parliament of accounts and reports laid before it in pursuance of subsection (1)(f).

(4) Scottish legislation may make further provision for the purpose of ensuring that persons who receive sums derived from the Fund are accountable including, in particular, provision for any person to whom subsection (1)(a) does not apply to be accountable for his expenditure and receipts in respect of functions for which he receives sums derived from the Fund.

(5) Persons (other than the Auditor General for Scotland) charged with the exercise of any function mentioned in subsection (2) or other like function conferred by Scottish legislation shall not, in the exercise of that or any ancillary function, be subject to the direction or control of any member of the Scottish Executive or of the Parliament.

(6) Scottish legislation may not require any cross-border public authority to prepare accounts if any other legislation requires—

(a) the authority to prepare accounts of its expenditure and receipts, and

(b) the accounts to be examined, certified and reported on by the Auditor General for Scotland, the Comptroller and Auditor General or a person appointed by either of them.

(7) Subsection (2)(b) does not apply to accounts prepared by the Auditor General for Scotland.

(8) This section does not require Scottish legislation to impose any requirement which is imposed by any other legislation.

(9) In this section—

"parliamentary accounts" means—

(a) any accounts prepared in pursuance of subsection (1)(a) or (b), and

(b) any accounts referred to in subsection (6) which are required to be examined, certified and reported on by the Auditor General for Scotland or any person appointed by him,

"Scottish legislation" means provision made by or under an Act of the Scottish Parliament and "other legislation" means provision made by any other enactment.

71 Existing debt

(1) Subsections (2) to (4) apply where—

(a) power to lend money under a provision of a pre-commencement enactment was exercised by the Secretary of State,

(b) the sums required by him for the exercise of the power were issued by the Treasury out of the National Loans Fund, and

(c) the power is exercisable by the Scottish Ministers by virtue of section 53, or would have been so exercisable but for the repeal of the pre-commencement enactment.

(2) Any amount payable by way of repayment of or interest on the loan shall be paid to the Scottish Ministers and into the Scottish Consolidated Fund (instead of to the Secretary of State and into the National Loans Fund).

(3) Amounts equal to those which are to be received by the Scottish Ministers in repayment of principal shall be treated as being amounts of advances made on the commencement of this section to the Scottish Ministers by the Secretary of State.

(4) Such advances shall be repaid to the Secretary of State at such times and by such methods, and interest on them shall be paid to him at such rates and at such times, as the Treasury may from time to time determine.

(5) Subsection (6) applies to any amount outstanding immediately before the commencement of this subsection in respect of the principal of the sum treated by virtue of section 2(3) of the Government Trading Funds Act 1973 as issued to the Registers of Scotland Executive Agency Trading Fund on the day on which the order establishing that fund came into force ("the issue date").

(6) The Secretary of State may, with the agreement of the Treasury, by order provide—

(a) for the amount to be treated as an advance made by him to the Scottish Ministers on the issue date, and

(b) for the advance to be repaid to him at such times and by such methods, and for interest on the advance to be paid to him at such rates and at such times, as were determined by the Treasury under section 2B(3) of that Act in respect of the sum referred to in subsection (5).

(7) Sums required to be paid under subsection (4) or (6) shall be charged on the Scottish Consolidated Fund.

(8) Sums received under subsection (4) or (6) shall be paid into the National Loans Fund.

72 Accounts of loans to the Scottish Ministers

The Secretary of State shall, for each financial year—

(a) prepare, in such form and manner as the Treasury may direct, an account of sums paid and received by him under sections 66, 67 and 71, and

(b) send the account to the Comptroller and Auditor General not later than the end of November in the following financial year,

and the Comptroller and Auditor General shall examine, certify and report on the account and shall lay copies of it and of his report before each House of Parliament.

PART IV

THE TAX-VARYING POWER

73 Power to fix basic rate for Scottish taxpayers

(1) Subject to section 74, this section applies for any year of assessment for which income tax is charged if—

(a) the Parliament has passed a resolution providing for the percentage determined to be the basic rate for that year to be increased or reduced for Scottish taxpayers in accordance with the resolution,

(b) the increase or reduction provided for is confined to an increase or reduction by a number not exceeding three which is specified in the resolution and is either a whole number or half of a whole number, and

(c) the resolution has not been cancelled by a subsequent resolution of the Parliament.

(2) Where this section applies for any year of assessment the Income Tax Acts (excluding this Part) shall have effect in relation to the income of Scottish taxpayers as if any rate determined by the Parliament of the United Kingdom to be the basic rate for that year were increased or reduced in accordance with the resolution of the Scottish Parliament.

(3) In subsection (2) the reference to the income of Scottish taxpayers does not include a reference to any income of Scottish taxpayers which, had it been income for the year 1998-99, would have been income to which section 1A of the Income and Corporation Taxes Act 1988 (income from savings and distributions) applied for that year.

(4) In this section—

(a) a reference, in relation to any year of assessment, to income tax being charged for that year includes a reference to the passing of a PCTA resolution that provides for the charging of that tax for that year, and

(b) a reference, in relation to a year of assessment, to the determination by the Parliament of the United Kingdom of a rate to be the basic rate for that year includes a reference to the passing of a PCTA resolution specifying a percentage to be the basic rate for that year.

(5) In this section "a PCTA resolution" means a resolution of the House of Commons containing such a declaration as is mentioned in section 1(2)(b) of the Provisional Collection of Taxes Act 1968.

74 Supplemental provision with respect to resolutions

(1) This section applies to any resolution of the Parliament ("a tax-varying resolution") which—

(a) provides, in accordance with section 73, for an increase or reduction for Scottish taxpayers of the basic rate for any year of assessment, or

(b) cancels a previous resolution of the Parliament providing for such an increase or reduction.

(2) Subject to subsection (3), a tax-varying resolution—

(a) must be expressed so as to relate to no more than a single year of assessment beginning after, but no more than twelve months after, the passing of the resolution, but

(b) shall have effect in relation to a determination by the Parliament of the United Kingdom of the rate to be the basic rate for that year irrespective of whether that determination had been made at the time of the passing of the resolution.

(3) Subsection (2) shall not prevent a tax-varying resolution relating to any year of assessment from being passed and having effect where—

(a) a determination by the Parliament of the United Kingdom of the rate to be the basic rate for that year is made after, or less than a month before, the beginning of that year,

(b) that determination is not confined to the passing of the enactment by which a determination of the same rate by a PCTA resolution is ratified, and

(c) the tax-varying resolution is passed within the period of one month beginning with the day of the making by the Parliament of the United Kingdom of its determination.

(4) Where, in a case to which subsection (3) applies, a tax-varying resolution is passed after the beginning of the year of assessment to which it relates—

(a) the resolution shall have effect as from the beginning of that year, and

(b) all such payments, repayments, deductions and other adjustments shall be made as are required to restore the position to what it would have been if the resolution had been passed before the beginning of that year.

(5) Standing orders shall ensure that only a member of the Scottish Executive may move a motion for a tax-varying resolution.

(6) A tax-varying resolution shall not be passed so as to have effect in relation to any year of assessment before the year 2000-01.

(7) Subsections (4) and (5) of section 73 apply for the purposes of this section as they apply for the purposes of that section.

75 Scottish taxpayers

(1) For the purposes of this Part a person is a Scottish taxpayer in relation to any year of assessment if—

(a) he is an individual who, for income tax purposes, is treated as resident in the United Kingdom in that year, and

(b) Scotland is the part of the United Kingdom with which he has the closest connection during that year.

(2) For the purposes of this section an individual who is treated for income tax purposes as resident in the United Kingdom in any year of assessment has his closest connection with Scotland during that year if, but only if, one or more of the following paragraphs applies in his case—

(a) he is an individual to whom subsection (3) applies for that year,

(b) the number of days which he spends in Scotland in that year is equal to or exceeds the number of days in that year which he spends elsewhere in the United Kingdom,

(c) he is an individual who, for the whole or any part of that year, is a member of Parliament for a constituency in Scotland, a member of the European Parliament for Scotland or a member of the Scottish Parliament.

(3) This subsection applies to an individual for a year of assessment if—

(a) he spends at least a part of that year in Scotland,

(b) for at least a part of the time that he spends in Scotland in that year, his principal UK home is located in Scotland and he makes use of it as a place of residence, and

(c) the times in that year when Scotland is where his principal UK home is located comprise (in aggregate) at least as much of that year as the times (if any) in that year when the location of his principal UK home is not in Scotland.

(4) For the purposes of this section—

(a) an individual spends a day in Scotland if, but only if, he is in Scotland at the end of that day, and

(b) an individual spends a day elsewhere in the United Kingdom if, but only if, he is in the United Kingdom at the end of that day and it is not a day that he spends in Scotland.

(5) For the purposes of this section an individual's principal UK home at any time is located in Scotland if at that time—

(a) he is an individual with a place of residence in Scotland, and

(b) in the case of an individual with two or more places of residence in the United Kingdom, Scotland is the location of such one of those places as at that time is his main place of residence in the United Kingdom.

(6) In this section "place" includes a place on board a vessel or other means of transport.

76 Changes to income tax structure

(1) This section applies where—

(a) there has been a proposal for the modification of any provision made by or under the Income Tax Acts,

(b) that proposal is one made and published by the Treasury or the Board, or (without having been so made and published) appears to the Treasury to be a proposal to which effect is likely to be given by Act of Parliament, and

(c) it appears to the Treasury that the proposed modification would have a significant effect on the practical extent for any year of assessment of the Parliament's tax-varying powers.

(2) It shall be the duty of the Treasury, as soon as reasonably practicable after the publication of the proposal, or (as the case may be) as soon as reasonably practicable after it first appears to the Treasury that the proposal is likely to be enacted, to lay before the House of Commons—

(a) a statement of whether, in the Treasury's opinion, an amendment of the Parliament's tax-varying powers is required as a consequence of the proposal, and

(b) if in their opinion an amendment of those powers is required, the Treasury's proposals for amending those powers.

(3) Any proposals for amending the Parliament's tax-varying powers that are laid before the House of Commons by the Treasury under this section—

(a) must be confined to income tax,

(b) must appear to the Treasury to satisfy the conditions set out in subsections (4) and (5), and

(c) must not contain any proposal for the Parliament's tax-varying powers to be exercisable in relation to the taxation of income from savings or distributions.

(4) The first condition mentioned in subsection (3)(b) is that the proposals would secure—

(a) so far as possible, and

(b) after making due allowance for annual changes in the retail prices index,

that the practical extent of the Parliament's tax-varying powers would remain broadly the same from year to year as it would be if (apart from any resolution of the Parliament) the law relating to income tax were the same from year to year as it was in relation to the year 1997-98.

(5) The second condition so mentioned is that the proposals would not enable the Parliament's tax-varying powers to be exercised for any year of assessment so as to have an effect on the levels of the after-tax income of Scottish taxpayers generally that would be significantly different from the effect their exercise could have had in any previous year of assessment.

(6) References in this section to the practical extent of the Parliament's tax-varying powers are references to the amounts of income tax for any year of assessment which appear to be or (as the case may be) to have been the maximum amounts capable of being raised and foregone in that year in pursuance of a resolution of the Parliament.

(7) In this section "income from savings or distributions" means income which, had it been income for the year 1998-99, would have been income to which section 1A of the Income and Corporation Taxes Act 1988 applied for that year.

77 Accounting for additional Scottish tax

(1) Where the basic rate for any year of assessment is increased for Scottish taxpayers by a resolution of the Parliament, it shall be the duty of the Board to pay amounts into the Scottish Consolidated Fund in accordance with this section.

(2) The amounts of the payments to be made by the Board under this section, and the times at which they are to be made, shall be determined by the Board and notified to the Scottish Ministers as soon as reasonably practicable after the passing of the resolution providing for the increase to which they relate.

(3) Any determination made by the Board under subsection (2) for any year of assessment shall be such as appears to the Board to be necessary for securing that, in the course of that year, amounts are paid into the Scottish Consolidated Fund which are equal in total to the amount estimated by the Board to represent the proportion of the income tax receipts for that year that is properly attributable to a resolution of the Parliament.

(4) For the purposes of this section the Board shall make and maintain arrangements as to—

(a) the manner of estimating the proportion of the income tax receipts for a year of assessment that is properly attributable to a resolution of the Parliament,

(b) the circumstances and manner in which an estimate of that proportion or of those receipts may be revised before or in the course of the year of assessment to which it relates,

(c) the manner of determining the amount of each payment to be made in respect of any such estimate, and

(d) the times at which, and manner in which, those amounts are to be paid by the Board into the Scottish Consolidated Fund.

(5) Arrangements under subsection (4) may include provision for the making of adjustments to the amounts paid by the Board where any estimate made for the purposes of this section in respect of any year of assessment (whether the current year or a previous year) turns out to have been inaccurate.

(6) Before making or modifying any arrangements under subsection (4) or (5), the Board shall consult with the Scottish Ministers.

(7) In this section "income tax receipts", in relation to any year of assessment, means so much as is referable to income tax charged for that year of any sums which, disregarding both—

(a) subsection (8), and

(b) any regulations or direction made or given by the Treasury,

are sums that have to be paid into the Consolidated Fund under section 10 of the Exchequer and Audit Departments Act 1866 (gross revenues of Board's department to be paid into that Fund after the making of specified deductions).

(8) Sums required by the Board for making payments under this section shall be paid out of the gross revenues of the Board's department; and, accordingly, those sums shall be treated as included in the amounts to be deducted from those revenues before they are paid into the Consolidated Fund under section 10 of the Exchequer and Audit Departments Act 1866.

78 Effect of tax reduction for Scottish taxpayers

(1) Where the basic rate for any year of assessment is reduced for Scottish taxpayers by a resolution of the Parliament, payments to the Board in accordance with this section shall be charged on the Scottish Consolidated Fund.

(2) The amounts of the payments to be made out of the Scottish Consolidated Fund under this section, and the times at which they are to be made, shall be determined by the Board and notified to the Scottish Ministers as soon as reasonably practicable after the passing of the resolution providing for the reduction to which they relate.

(3) Any determination made by the Board under subsection (2) for any year of assessment shall be such as appears to the Board to be necessary for securing that in the course of that year amounts are paid to the Board which are equal in total to the amount estimated by the Board to represent the shortfall in income tax receipts for that year that is properly attributable to a resolution of the Parliament.

(4) For the purposes of this section the Board shall make and maintain arrangements as to—

(a) the manner of estimating the shortfall in income tax receipts for any year of assessment that is properly attributable to a resolution of the Parliament,

(b) the circumstances and manner in which an estimate of that shortfall may be revised before or in the course of the year of assessment to which it relates,

(c) the manner of determining the amount of each payment to be made in respect of any such estimate, and

(d) the times at which, and manner in which, those amounts are to be paid to the Board.

(5) Arrangements under subsection (4) may include provision for the making of adjustments to the amounts paid to the Board where any estimate made for the purposes of this section in respect of any year of assessment (whether the current year or a previous year) turns out to have been inaccurate.

(6) Before making or modifying any arrangements under subsection (4) or (5), the Board shall consult with the Scottish Ministers.

(7) In this section "income tax receipts" has the same meaning as in section 77.

(8) The sums paid to the Board under this section shall be treated for the purposes of section 10 of the Exchequer and Audit Departments Act 1866 (payment, after the making of the specified deductions, of gross revenues into the Consolidated Fund) as comprised in their department's gross revenues.

79 Supplemental powers to modify enactments

(1) The Treasury may by order make such modifications of any enactment as they consider necessary or expedient in consequence of—

(a) the fact that the Parliament has, or is to have, the power to pass a tax-varying resolution, or

(b) the fact (where it is the case) that the Parliament has passed such a resolution.

(2) The Treasury may by order make provision—

(a) excluding the operation of section 73(2) in relation to any enactment, and

(b) making any such other modifications of any enactment as they consider necessary or expedient in connection with, or for the purposes of, any such exclusion.

(3) Without prejudice to the generality of the powers conferred by the preceding provisions of this section, an order under this section may provide that, where any tax-varying resolution relating to any year of assessment is passed, that resolution does not require any change in the amounts repayable or deductible under section 203 of the Income and Corporation Taxes Act 1988 (PAYE) between—

(a) the beginning of that year, and

(b) such day falling after the passing of the resolution as may be specified in the order.

(4) An order under this section may, to the extent that the Treasury consider it to be appropriate, take effect retrospectively from the beginning of the year of assessment in which it is made.

(5) In this section "tax-varying resolution" has the same meaning as in section 74.

80 Reimbursement of expenses

The Scottish Ministers may reimburse any Minister of the Crown or government department for administrative expenses incurred by virtue of this Part at any time after the passing of this Act by the Minister or department.

PART V

MISCELLANEOUS AND GENERAL

Remuneration of members of the Parliament and Executive

81 Remuneration of members of the Parliament and Executive

(1) The Parliament shall make provision for the payment of salaries to members of the Parliament and members of the Scottish Executive.

(2) The Parliament may make provision for the payment of allowances to members of the Parliament or members of the Scottish Executive.

(3) The Parliament may make provision for the payment of pensions, gratuities or allowances to, or in respect of, any person who—

(a) has ceased to be a member of the Parliament or the Scottish Executive, or

(b) has ceased to hold such office, employment or other post in connection with the Parliament or the Scottish Executive as the Parliament may determine but continues to be a member of the Parliament or the Scottish Executive.

(4) Such provision may, in particular, include provision for—

(a) contributions or payments towards provision for such pensions, gratuities or allowances,

(b) the establishment and administration (whether by the Parliamentary corporation or otherwise) of one or more pension schemes.

(5) In this section "provision" includes provision—

(a) by an Act of the Scottish Parliament, or

(b) by a resolution of the Parliament conferring functions on the Parliamentary corporation;

and references to a member of the Scottish Executive include a junior Scottish Minister.

82 Limits on salaries of members of the Parliament

(1) The Parliament shall ensure that the amount of salary payable to a member of the Parliament in accordance with section 81 is reduced if any salary is payable to him—

(a) pursuant to a resolution (or combination of resolutions) of either House of Parliament relating to the remuneration of members of that House, or

(b) under section 1 of the European Parliament (Pay and Pensions) Act 1979 (remuneration of United Kingdom MEPs).

(2) The Parliament shall ensure that the amount of salary is reduced—

(a) to a particular proportion of what it would otherwise be or to a particular amount, or

(b) by the amount of any salary payable to the member as mentioned in subsection (1)(a) or (b), by a particular proportion of that amount or by some other particular amount.

83 Remuneration: supplementary

(1) The Parliament shall ensure that information concerning sums paid as salaries, allowances, pensions or gratuities of the kind mentioned in section 81 is published for each financial year.

(2) No payment of salary or allowances of the kind mentioned in section 81(1) or (2) shall be made to a person who is required by section 84 to take an oath unless he has done so.

(3) Subsection (2) does not affect any entitlement to payments in respect of the period before the person concerned took the oath once he has done so.

(4) For the purposes of sections 81 and 82, a person who is a member of the Parliament immediately before the Parliament is dissolved shall be treated—

(a) if he continues to hold office by virtue of section 19(2) or paragraph 1 of Schedule 2, as if he were such a member until the end of the day on which he ceases to hold such office, and

(b) if he does not fall within paragraph (a) but is nominated as a candidate at the subsequent general election, as if he were such a member until the end of the day on which the election is held.

(5) Different provision may be made under section 81 or 82 for different cases.

Other provision about members of the Parliament etc.

84 Oaths

(1) A person who is returned as a member of the Parliament shall take the oath of allegiance (whether or not he has taken the oath after being returned on a previous occasion or otherwise than as a member of the Parliament).

(2) He shall do so at a meeting of the Parliament and shall not take part in any other proceedings of the Parliament until he has done so.

(3) If he has not done so within the period of two months beginning with the day on which he was returned, or such longer period as the Parliament may have allowed before the end of that period, he shall cease to be a member of the Parliament (so that his seat is vacant).

(4) Each member of the Scottish Executive shall on appointment—

(a) take the official oath in the form provided by the Promissory Oaths Act 1868, and

(b) take the oath of allegiance.

(5) Each junior Scottish Minister shall on appointment take the oath of allegiance.

(6) Subsections (4) and (5) do not require a member of the Parliament to take the oath of allegiance again if he has already done so in compliance with his duty as a member.

(7) In this section, references to taking the oath of allegiance are to taking it in the form provided by the Promissory Oaths Act 1868.

85 Exemption from jury service

(1) In Part III of Schedule 1 to the Juries Act 1974 (persons excusable as of right from jury service), after the entries under the heading "Parliament" there is inserted—

"Scottish Parliament and Scottish Executive

Members of the Scottish Parliament.

Members of the Scottish Executive.

Junior Scottish Ministers."

(2) In Part III of Schedule 1 to the Law Reform (Miscellaneous Provisions) (Scotland) Act 1980 (persons excusable as of right from jury service), after the entries in Group A there is inserted—

"GROUP AB

Scottish Parliament and Scottish Executive

(a) members of the Scottish Parliament;

(b) members of the Scottish Executive; and

(c) junior Scottish Ministers."

Arrangements at Westminster

86 Scottish representation at Westminster

(1) Schedule 2 to the Parliamentary Constituencies Act 1986 (rules for redistribution of seats) is amended as follows.

(2) Rule 1(2) (Scotland to have not less than 71 constituencies) is omitted.

(3) After rule 3 there is inserted—

"3A A constituency which includes the Orkney Islands or the Shetland Islands shall not include the whole or any part of a local government area other than the Orkney Islands and the Shetland Islands."; and in rule 4, for "3" there is substituted "3A".

(4) In applying rule 5 (electoral quotas for each part of the United Kingdom) to Scotland for the purposes of the first report of the Boundary Commission for Scotland to be submitted under section 3(1) of that Act after the commencement of this subsection, "electoral quota" means the number which, on the enumeration date in relation to that report, is the electoral quota for England.

(5) In paragraph 7 (Commissions do not have to give full effect to all rules), after "rules" there is inserted "(except rule 3A)".

87 The Advocate General for Scotland

(1) In Schedule 2 to the House of Commons Disqualification Act 1975 (Ministerial offices) and Part III of Schedule 1 to the Ministerial and other Salaries Act 1975 (salaries of the Law Officers), after the entry for the Solicitor General there is inserted—

"Advocate General for Scotland".

(2) The validity of anything done in relation to the Advocate General is not affected by a vacancy in that office.

(3) If that office is vacant or the Advocate General is for any reason unable to act, his functions shall be exercisable by such other Minister of the Crown as the Prime Minister may determine in writing.

Cross-border public authorities

88 Cross-border public authorities: initial status

(1) Sections 53 and 118 to 121 shall not apply in relation to any function which is specifically exercisable in relation to a cross-border public authority; and section 118 shall not apply in relation to any function of such an authority.

(2) A Minister of the Crown shall consult the Scottish Ministers before he exercises, in relation to a cross-border public authority, any specific function—

- (a) which relates to any appointment or removal of the cross-border public authority concerned or of any members or office-holders of the cross-border public authority concerned, or
- (b) whose exercise might affect Scotland otherwise than wholly in relation to reserved matters.

(3) Any cross-border public authority or other person which is required by a pre-commencement enactment or a prerogative instrument to lay any report relating to a cross-border public authority before Parliament or either House of Parliament shall also lay the report before the Scottish Parliament.

(4) Subsections (1) to (3) are subject to any Order in Council made under section 89.

(5) In this Act "cross-border public authority" means any body, government department, office or office-holder specified in an Order in Council made by Her Majesty under this section.

(6) Such an Order may only specify a body, government department, office or office-holder which (at the time when the Order is made) has, in addition to other functions, functions which are exercisable in or as regards Scotland and do not relate to reserved matters.

(7) In this section—

"office-holder" includes employee or other post-holder,

"report" includes accounts and any statement.

89 Power to adapt etc. cross-border public authorities

(1) Her Majesty may by Order in Council make such provision in relation to a cross-border public authority as She considers necessary or expedient in consequence of this Act.

(2) Such provision may, in particular, include provision—

- (a) modifying any function of a cross-border public authority or of a Minister of the Crown in relation to such an authority,

(b) conferring any function on a cross-border public authority or on a Minister of the Crown or the Scottish Ministers in relation to such an authority,

(c) modifying the constitution of a cross-border public authority,

(d) modifying the application of section 56(4) or 88(1), (2) or (3),

(e) for any function to be exercisable by the Scottish Ministers instead of by a Minister of the Crown, or by the one concurrently with the other, or by both jointly or by either with the agreement of or after consultation with the other,

(f) apportioning any assets or liabilities,

(g) imposing, or enabling the imposition of, any limits or other restrictions in addition to or in substitution for existing limits or restrictions,

(h) providing for sums to be charged on or payable out of, or paid into, the Scottish Consolidated Fund (instead of or in addition to payments into or out of the Consolidated Fund or the National Loans Fund or out of money provided by Parliament),

(i) requiring payments, with or without interest, to a Minister of the Crown or into the Consolidated Fund or National Loans Fund.

(3) No recommendation shall be made to Her Majesty in Council to make an Order under this section unless the cross-border public authority concerned has been consulted.

90 Power to transfer property of cross-border public authorities

(1) This section applies if an Act of the Scottish Parliament provides for any functions of a cross-border public authority to be no longer exercisable in or as regards Scotland.

(2) Her Majesty may by Order in Council provide—

(a) for the transfer of any property to which this section applies, or

(b) for any person to have such rights or interests in relation to any property to which this section applies as Her Majesty considers appropriate (whether in connection with a transfer or otherwise).

(3) This section applies to property belonging to the cross-border public authority concerned which appears to Her Majesty—

(a) to be held or used wholly or partly for or in connection with the exercise of any of the functions concerned, or

(b) not to be within paragraph (a) but, when last held or used for or in connection with the exercise of any function, to have been so held or used for or in connection with the exercise of any of the functions concerned.

(4) Her Majesty may by Order in Council provide for the transfer of any liabilities—

(a) to which the cross-border public authority concerned is subject, and

(b) which appear to Her Majesty to have been incurred wholly or partly for or in connection with the exercise of any of the functions concerned.

(5) No recommendation shall be made to Her Majesty in Council to make an Order under this section unless the cross-border public authority concerned has been consulted.

Miscellaneous

91 Maladministration

(1) The Parliament shall make provision for the investigation of relevant complaints made to its members in respect of any action taken by or on behalf of—

(a) a member of the Scottish Executive in the exercise of functions conferred on the Scottish Ministers, or

(b) any other office-holder in the Scottish Administration.

(2) For the purposes of subsection (1), a complaint is a relevant complaint if it is a complaint of a kind which could be investigated under the Parliamentary Commissioner Act 1967 if it were made to a member of the House of Commons in respect of a government department or other authority to which that Act applies.

(3) The Parliament may make provision for the investigation of complaints in respect of—

(a) any action taken by or on behalf of an office-holder in the Scottish Administration,

(b) any action taken by or on behalf of the Parliamentary corporation,

(c) any action taken by or on behalf of a Scottish public authority with mixed functions or no reserved functions, or

(d) any action concerning Scotland and not relating to reserved matters which is taken by or on behalf of a cross-border public authority.

(4) In making provision of the kind required by subsection (1), the Parliament shall have regard (among other things) to the Act of 1967.

(5) Sections 53 and 117 to 121 shall not apply in relation to functions conferred by or under the Act of 1967.

(6) In this section—

"action" includes failure to act (and related expressions shall be read accordingly),

"provision" means provision by an Act of the Scottish Parliament;

and the references to the Act of 1967 are to that Act as it has effect on the commencement of this section.

92 Queen's Printer for Scotland

(1) There shall be a Queen's Printer for Scotland who shall—

(a) exercise the Queen's Printer functions in relation to Acts of the Scottish Parliament and subordinate legislation to which this section applies, and

(b) exercise any other functions conferred on her by this Act or any other enactment.

(2) In subsection (1), "the Queen's Printer functions" means the printing functions in relation to Acts of Parliament and subordinate legislation of the Queen's Printer of Acts of Parliament.

(3) The Queen's Printer for Scotland shall also on behalf of Her Majesty exercise Her rights and privileges in connection with—

(a) Crown copyright in Acts of the Scottish Parliament,

(b) Crown copyright in subordinate legislation to which this section applies,

(c) Crown copyright in any existing or future works (other than subordinate legislation) made in the exercise of a function which is exercisable by any office-holder in, or member of the staff of, the Scottish Administration (or would be so exercisable if the function had not ceased to exist),

(d) other copyright assigned to Her Majesty in works made in connection with the exercise of functions by any such office-holder or member.

(4) This section applies to subordinate legislation made, confirmed or approved—

(a) by a member of the Scottish Executive,

(b) by a Scottish public authority with mixed functions or no reserved functions, or

(c) within devolved competence by a person other than a Minister of the Crown or such a member or authority.

(5) The Queen's Printer of Acts of Parliament shall hold the office of Queen's Printer for Scotland.

(6) References in this Act to a Scottish public authority include the Queen's Printer for Scotland.

93 Agency arrangements

(1) A Minister of the Crown may make arrangements for any of his specified functions to be exercised on his behalf by the Scottish Ministers; and the Scottish Ministers may make arrangements for any of their specified functions to be exercised on their behalf by a Minister of the Crown.

(2) An arrangement under this section does not affect a person's responsibility for the exercise of his functions.

(3) In this section—

"functions" does not include a function of making, confirming or approving subordinate legislation,

"Minister of the Crown" includes government department,

"specified" means specified in an Order in Council made by Her Majesty under this subsection;

and this section applies to the Lord Advocate as it applies to the Scottish Ministers.

94 Private legislation

(1) This section applies where a pre-commencement enactment makes provision which has the effect of—

(a) requiring any order to be confirmed by Act of Parliament, or

(b) requiring any order (within the meaning of the Statutory Orders (Special Procedure) Act 1945) to be subject to special parliamentary procedure,

and power to make, confirm or approve the order in question is exercisable by the Scottish Ministers by virtue of section 53.

(2) The provision shall have effect, so far as it relates to the exercise of the power to make, confirm or approve the order by virtue of section 53, as if it required the order—

(a) to be confirmed by an Act of the Scottish Parliament, or

(b) (as the case may be) to be subject to such special procedure as may be provided by or under such an Act.

95 Appointment and removal of judges

(1) It shall continue to be for the Prime Minister to recommend to Her Majesty the appointment of a person as Lord President of the Court of Session or Lord Justice Clerk.

(2) The Prime Minister shall not recommend to Her Majesty the appointment of any person who has not been nominated by the First Minister for such appointment.

(3) Before nominating persons for such appointment the First Minister shall consult the Lord President and the Lord Justice Clerk (unless, in either case, the office is vacant).

(4) It is for the First Minister, after consulting the Lord President, to recommend to Her Majesty the appointment of a person as—

(a) a judge of the Court of Session (other than the Lord President or the Lord Justice Clerk), or

(b) a sheriff principal or a sheriff.

(5) The First Minister shall comply with any requirement in relation to—

(a) a nomination under subsection (2), or

(b) a recommendation under subsection (4),

imposed by virtue of any enactment.

(6) A judge of the Court of Session and the Chairman of the Scottish Land Court may be removed from office only by Her Majesty; and any recommendation to Her Majesty for such removal shall be made by the First Minister.

(7) The First Minister shall make such a recommendation if (and only if) the Parliament, on a motion made by the First Minister, resolves that such a recommendation should be made.

(8) Provision shall be made for a tribunal constituted by the First Minister to investigate and report on whether a judge of the Court of Session or the Chairman of the Scottish Land Court is unfit for office by reason of inability, neglect of duty or misbehaviour and for the report to be laid before the Parliament.

(9) Such provision shall include provision—

(a) for the constitution of the tribunal by the First Minister when requested by the Lord President to do so and in such other circumstances as the First Minister thinks fit, and

(b) for the appointment to chair the tribunal of a member of the Judicial Committee who holds or has held any of the offices referred to in section 103(2),

and may include provision for suspension from office.

(10) The First Minister may make a motion under subsection (7) only if—

(a) he has received from a tribunal constituted in pursuance of subsection (8) a written report concluding that the person in question is unfit for office by reason of inability, neglect of duty or misbehaviour and giving reasons for that conclusion,

(b) where the person in question is the Lord President or the Lord Justice Clerk, he has consulted the Prime Minister, and

(c) he has complied with any other requirement imposed by virtue of any enactment.

(11) In subsections (8) to (10)—

"provision" means provision by or under an Act of the Scottish Parliament,

"tribunal" means a tribunal of at least three persons.

96 Provision of information to the Treasury

(1) The Treasury may require the Scottish Ministers to provide, within such period as the Treasury may reasonably specify, such information, in such form and prepared in such manner, as the Treasury may reasonably specify.

(2) If the information is not in their possession or under their control, their duty under subsection (1) is to take all reasonable steps to comply with the requirement.

97 Assistance for opposition parties

(1) Her Majesty may by Order in Council provide for the Parliamentary corporation to make payments to registered political parties for the purpose of assisting members of the Parliament who are connected with such parties to perform their Parliamentary duties.

(2) The corporation shall not make any payment to a party in pursuance of such an Order if any of the members of the Parliament who are connected with the party are also members of the Scottish Executive or junior Scottish Ministers.

(3) But such an Order may, in any circumstances specified in the Order, require the fact that any members who are connected with a party are also members of the Scottish Executive or junior Scottish Ministers to be disregarded.

(4) Such an Order may determine the circumstances in which a member of the Parliament and a registered political party are to be regarded for the purposes of this section as connected.

Juridical

98 Devolution issues

Schedule 6 (which makes provision in relation to devolution issues) shall have effect.

99 Rights and liabilities of the Crown in different capacities

(1) Rights and liabilities may arise between the Crown in right of Her Majesty's Government in the United Kingdom and the Crown in right of the Scottish Administration by virtue of a contract, by operation of law or by virtue of an enactment as they may arise between subjects.

(2) Property and liabilities may be transferred between the Crown in one of those capacities and the Crown in the other capacity as they may be transferred between

subjects; and they may together create, vary or extinguish any property or liability as subjects may.

(3) Proceedings in respect of—

(a) any property or liabilities to which the Crown in one of those capacities is entitled or subject under subsection (1) or (2), or

(b) the exercise of, or failure to exercise, any function exercisable by an office-holder of the Crown in one of those capacities,

may be instituted by the Crown in either capacity; and the Crown in the other capacity may be a separate party in the proceedings.

(4) This section applies to a unilateral obligation as it applies to a contract.

(5) In this section—

"office-holder", in relation to the Crown in right of Her Majesty's Government in the United Kingdom, means any Minister of the Crown or other office-holder under the Crown in that capacity and, in relation to the Crown in right of the Scottish Administration, means any office-holder in the Scottish Administration,

"subject" means a person not acting on behalf of the Crown.

100 Human rights

(1) This Act does not enable a person—

(a) to bring any proceedings in a court or tribunal on the ground that an act is incompatible with the Convention rights, or

(b) to rely on any of the Convention rights in any such proceedings,

unless he would be a victim for the purposes of Article 34 of the Convention (within the meaning of the Human Rights Act 1998) if proceedings in respect of the act were brought in the European Court of Human Rights.

(2) Subsection (1) does not apply to the Lord Advocate, the Advocate General, the Attorney General or the Attorney General for Northern Ireland.

(3) This Act does not enable a court or tribunal to award any damages in respect of an act which is incompatible with any of the Convention rights which it could not award if section 8(3) and (4) of the Human Rights Act 1998 applied.

(4) In this section "act" means—

(a) making any legislation,

(b) any other act or failure to act, if it is the act or failure of a member of the Scottish Executive.

101 Interpretation of Acts of the Scottish Parliament etc

(1) This section applies to—

(a) any provision of an Act of the Scottish Parliament, or of a Bill for such an Act, and

(b) any provision of subordinate legislation made, confirmed or approved, or purporting to be made, confirmed or approved, by a member of the Scottish Executive,

which could be read in such a way as to be outside competence.

(2) Such a provision is to be read as narrowly as is required for it to be within competence, if such a reading is possible, and is to have effect accordingly.

(3) In this section "competence"—

(a) in relation to an Act of the Scottish Parliament, or a Bill for such an Act, means the legislative competence of the Parliament, and

(b) in relation to subordinate legislation, means the powers conferred by virtue of this Act.

102 Powers of courts or tribunals to vary retrospective decisions

(1) This section applies where any court or tribunal decides that—

(a) an Act of the Scottish Parliament or any provision of such an Act is not within the legislative competence of the Parliament, or

(b) a member of the Scottish Executive does not have the power to make, confirm or approve a provision of subordinate legislation that he has purported to make, confirm or approve.

(2) The court or tribunal may make an order—

(a) removing or limiting any retrospective effect of the decision, or

(b) suspending the effect of the decision for any period and on any conditions to allow the defect to be corrected.

(3) In deciding whether to make an order under this section, the court or tribunal shall (among other things) have regard to the extent to which persons who are not parties to the proceedings would otherwise be adversely affected.

(4) Where a court or tribunal is considering whether to make an order under this section, it shall order intimation of that fact to be given to—

(a) the Lord Advocate, and

(b) the appropriate law officer, where the decision mentioned in subsection (1) relates to a devolution issue (within the meaning of Schedule 6),

unless the person to whom the intimation would be given is a party to the proceedings.

(5) A person to whom intimation is given under subsection (4) may take part as a party in the proceedings so far as they relate to the making of the order.

(6) Paragraphs 36 and 37 of Schedule 6 apply with necessary modifications for the purposes of subsections (4) and (5) as they apply for the purposes of that Schedule.

(7) In this section—

"intimation" includes notice,

"the appropriate law officer" means—

(a) in relation to proceedings in Scotland, the Advocate General,

(b) in relation to proceedings in England and Wales, the Attorney General,

(c) in relation to proceedings in Northern Ireland, the Attorney General for Northern Ireland.

103 The Judicial Committee

(1) Any decision of the Judicial Committee in proceedings under this Act shall be stated in open court and shall be binding in all legal proceedings (other than proceedings before the Committee).

(2) No member of the Judicial Committee shall sit and act as a member of the Committee in proceedings under this Act unless he holds or has held—

(a) the office of a Lord of Appeal in Ordinary, or

(b) high judicial office as defined in section 25 of the Appellate Jurisdiction Act 1876 (ignoring for this purpose section 5 of the Appellate Jurisdiction Act 1887).

(3) Her Majesty may by Order in Council—

(a) confer on the Judicial Committee in relation to proceedings under this Act such powers as Her Majesty considers necessary or expedient,

(b) apply the Judicial Committee Act 1833 in relation to proceedings under this Act with exceptions or modifications,

(c) make rules for regulating the procedure in relation to proceedings under this Act before the Judicial Committee.

(4) In this section "proceedings under this Act" means proceedings on a question referred to the Judicial Committee under section 33 or proceedings under Schedule 6.

Supplementary powers

104 Power to make provision consequential on legislation of, or scrutinised by, the Parliament

(1) Subordinate legislation may make such provision as the person making the legislation considers necessary or expedient in consequence of any provision made by or under any Act of the Scottish Parliament or made by legislation mentioned in subsection (2).

(2) The legislation is subordinate legislation under an Act of Parliament made by—

(a) a member of the Scottish Executive,

(b) a Scottish public authority with mixed functions or no reserved functions, or

(c) any other person (not being a Minister of the Crown) if the function of making the legislation is exercisable within devolved competence.

105 Power to make provision consequential on this Act

Subordinate legislation may make such modifications in any pre-commencement enactment or prerogative instrument or any other instrument or document as appear to the person making the legislation necessary or expedient in consequence of this Act.

106 Power to adapt functions

(1) Subordinate legislation may make such provision (including, in particular, provision modifying a function exercisable by a Minister of the Crown) as the person making the legislation considers appropriate for the purpose of enabling or otherwise facilitating the transfer of a function to the Scottish Ministers by virtue of section 53 or 63.

(2) Subordinate legislation under subsection (1) may, in particular, provide for any function which—

(a) is not exercisable separately in or as regards Scotland to be so exercisable, or

(b) is not otherwise exercisable separately within devolved competence to be so exercisable.

(3) The reference in subsection (1) to the transfer of a function to the Scottish Ministers shall be read as including the sharing of a function with the Scottish Ministers or its other adaptation.

(4) No recommendation shall be made to Her Majesty in Council to make, and no Minister of the Crown shall make, subordinate legislation under this section which modifies a function of observing or implementing an obligation mentioned in subsection (5) unless the Scottish Ministers have been consulted about the modification.

(5) The obligation is an international obligation, or an obligation under Community law, to achieve a result defined by reference to a quantity (whether expressed as an amount, proportion or ratio or otherwise), where the quantity relates to the United Kingdom (or to an area including the United Kingdom or to an area consisting of a part of the United Kingdom which includes the whole or part of Scotland).

(6) If subordinate legislation under this section modifies a function of observing or implementing such an international obligation so that the function to be transferred to the Scottish Ministers relates only to achieving so much of the result to be achieved under the obligation as is specified in the legislation, references in section 58 to the international obligation are to be read as references to the requirement to achieve that much of the result.

(7) If subordinate legislation under this section modifies a function of observing or implementing such an obligation under Community law so that the function to be transferred to the Scottish Ministers relates only to achieving so much of the result to be achieved under the obligation as is specified in the legislation, references in sections 29(2)(d) and 57(2) and paragraph 1 of Schedule 6 to Community law are to be read as including references to the requirement to achieve that much of the result.

107 Legislative power to remedy ultra vires acts

Subordinate legislation may make such provision as the person making the legislation considers necessary or expedient in consequence of—

(a) an Act of the Scottish Parliament or any provision of an Act of the Scottish Parliament which is not, or may not be, within the legislative competence of the Parliament, or

(b) any purported exercise by a member of the Scottish Executive of his functions which is not, or may not be, an exercise or a proper exercise of those functions.

108 Agreed redistribution of functions exercisable by the Scottish Ministers etc

(1) Her Majesty may by Order in Council provide for any functions exercisable by a member of the Scottish Executive to be exercisable—

(a) by a Minister of the Crown instead of by the member of the Scottish Executive,

(b) by a Minister of the Crown concurrently with the member of the Scottish Executive, or

(c) by the member of the Scottish Executive only with the agreement of, or after consultation with, a Minister of the Crown.

(2) Where an Order is made under subsection (1)(a) or (b) in relation to a function of the Scottish Ministers, the First Minister or the Lord Advocate which is exercisable only with the agreement of, or after consultation with, any other of those persons, the function shall, unless the Order provides otherwise, be exercisable by the Minister of the Crown free from any such requirement.

(3) An Order under this section may, in particular, provide for any function exercisable by a Minister of the Crown by virtue of an Order under subsection (1)(a) or (b) to be exercisable subject to a requirement for the function to be exercised with the agreement of, or after consultation with, another person.

(4) This section does not apply to any retained functions of the Lord Advocate which fall within section 52(6)(a).

109 Agreed redistribution of property and liabilities

(1) Her Majesty may by Order in Council provide—

(a) for the transfer to a Minister of the Crown or government department of any property belonging to the Scottish Ministers or the Lord Advocate, or

(b) for a Minister of the Crown or government department to have such rights or interests in relation to any property belonging to the Scottish Ministers or the Lord Advocate as Her Majesty considers appropriate (whether in connection with a transfer or otherwise).

(2) Her Majesty may by Order in Council provide for the transfer to a Minister of the Crown or government department of any liabilities to which the Scottish Ministers or the Lord Advocate are subject.

(3) An Order in Council under this section may only be made in connection with any transfer or sharing of functions of a member of the Scottish Executive by virtue of section 108 or in any other circumstances in which Her Majesty considers it appropriate to do so for the purposes of this Act.

110 Scottish taxpayers for social security purposes

(1) The Secretary of State may by order provide for individuals of any description specified in the order to be treated for the purposes of any of the matters that are reserved matters by virtue of Head F of Part II of Schedule 5 as if they were, or were not, Scottish taxpayers.

(2) The Secretary of State may by order provide in relation to any year of assessment that, for those purposes, the basic rate in relation to the income of Scottish taxpayers shall be treated as being such rate as is specified in the order (instead of the rate increased or reduced for that year by virtue of any resolution of the Parliament in pursuance of section 73 passed after the beginning of the year).

(3) An order under this section may apply in respect of any individuals whether Scotland is the part of the United Kingdom with which they have the closest connection or not.

(4) In this section "Scottish taxpayer" has the same meaning as in Part IV.

111 Regulation of Tweed and Esk fisheries

(1) Her Majesty may by Order in Council make provision for or in connection with the conservation, management and exploitation of salmon, trout, eels and freshwater fish in the Border rivers.

(2) An Order under subsection (1) may—

(a) exclude the application of section 53 in relation to any Border rivers function,

(b) confer power to make subordinate legislation.

(3) In particular, provision may be made by such an Order—

(a) conferring any function on a Minister of the Crown, the Scottish Ministers or a public body in relation to the Border rivers,

(b) for any Border rivers function exercisable by any person to be exercisable instead by a person (or another person) mentioned in paragraph (a),

(c) for any Border rivers function exercisable by any person to be exercisable concurrently or jointly with, or with the agreement of or after consultation with, a person (or another person) mentioned in paragraph (a).

(4) In this section—

"the Border rivers" means the Rivers Tweed and Esk,

"Border rivers function" means a function conferred by any enactment, so far as exercisable in relation to the Border rivers,

"conservation", in relation to salmon, trout, eels and freshwater fish, includes the protection of their environment,

"eels", "freshwater fish", "salmon" and "trout" have the same meanings as in the Salmon and Freshwater Fisheries Act 1975,

"the River Tweed" has the same meaning as in section 39 of the Salmon and Freshwater Fisheries Act 1975,

"the River Esk" means the river of that name which, for part of its length, constitutes the border between England and Scotland including—

(a) its tributary streams (which for this purpose include the River Sark and its tributary streams), and

(b) such waters on the landward side of its estuary limits as are determined by an Order under subsection (1),

together with its banks;

and references to the Border rivers include any part of the Border rivers.

(5) An Order under subsection (1) may modify the definitions in subsection (4) of the River Tweed and the River Esk.

PART VI

SUPPLEMENTARY

Subordinate legislation

112 Subordinate legislation: general

(1) Any power to make subordinate legislation conferred by this Act shall, if no other provision is made as to the person by whom the power is exercisable, be exercisable by Her Majesty by Order in Council or by a Minister of the Crown by order.

(2) But the power to make subordinate legislation under section 129(1) providing—

(a) for the appropriation of sums forming part of the Scottish Consolidated Fund, or

(b) for sums received by any person to be appropriated in aid of sums appropriated as mentioned in paragraph (a),

shall be exercisable only by Her Majesty by Order in Council.

(3) References in this Act to an open power are to a power to which subsection (1) applies (and include a power to make subordinate legislation under section 129(1) whether or not the legislation makes provision as mentioned in subsection (2)).

(4) An Order in Council under an open power may revoke, amend or re-enact an order, as well as an Order in Council, under the power; and an order under an open power may revoke, amend or re-enact an Order in Council, as well as an order, under the power.

(5) Any power to make subordinate legislation conferred by this Act shall, in relation to its exercise by a Minister of the Crown or a member of the Scottish Executive, be exercisable by statutory instrument.

113 Subordinate legislation: scope of powers

(1) References in this section to a power are to an open power and to any other power to make subordinate legislation conferred by this Act which is exercisable by Her Majesty in Council or by a Minister of the Crown, and include a power as extended by this section.

(2) A power may be exercised so as to make different provision for different purposes.

(3) A power (as well as being exercisable in relation to all cases to which it extends) may be exercised in relation to—

(a) those cases subject to specified exceptions, or

(b) any particular case or class of case.

(4) A power includes power to make—

(a) any supplementary, incidental or consequential provision, and

(b) any transitory, transitional or saving provision,

which the person making the legislation considers necessary or expedient.

(5) A power may be exercised by modifying—

(a) any enactment or prerogative instrument,

(b) any other instrument or document,

if the subordinate legislation (or a statutory instrument containing it) would be subject to any of the types of procedure referred to in Schedule 7.

(6) But a power to modify enactments does not (unless otherwise stated) extend to making modifications of this Act or subordinate legislation under it.

(7) A power may be exercised so as to make provision for the delegation of functions.

(8) A power includes power to make provision for sums to be payable out of the Scottish Consolidated Fund or charged on the Fund.

(9) A power includes power to make provision for the payment of sums out of money provided by Parliament or for sums to be charged on and paid out of the Consolidated Fund.

(10) A power may not be exercised so as to create any criminal offence punishable—

(a) on summary conviction, with imprisonment for a period exceeding three months or with a fine exceeding the amount specified as level 5 on the standard scale,

(b) on conviction on indictment, with a period of imprisonment exceeding two years.

(11) The fact that a power is conferred does not prejudice the extent of any other power.

114 Subordinate legislation: particular provisions

(1) A power to make subordinate legislation conferred by any of the following provisions of this Act may be exercised by modifying any enactment comprised in or made under this Act (except Schedules 4 and 5): sections 89, 104, 107, 108 and 129(1).

(2) The reference in subsection (1) to a power to make subordinate legislation includes a power as extended by section 113.

(3) A power to make subordinate legislation conferred by any of the following provisions of this Act may be exercised so as to make provision having retrospective effect: sections 30, 58(4), 104 and 107.

115 Subordinate legislation: procedure

(1) Schedule 7 (which determines the procedure which is to apply to subordinate legislation under this Act in relation to each House of Parliament and the Scottish Parliament) shall have effect.

(2) In spite of the fact that that Schedule provides for subordinate legislation under a particular provision of this Act (or the statutory instrument containing it) to be subject to any type of procedure in relation to the Parliament, the provision conferring the power to make that legislation may be brought into force at any time after the passing of this Act.

(3) Accordingly, any subordinate legislation (or the statutory instrument containing it) made in the exercise of the power in the period beginning with that time and ending immediately before the principal appointed day is to be subject to such other type of procedure (if any) as may be specified in subordinate legislation made under section 129(1).

116 Transfer of property: supplementary

(1) This section applies in relation to subordinate legislation under section 60, 62, 90 or 109 or paragraph 2 of Schedule 2.

(2) Any such subordinate legislation may, in particular—

(a) provide for the creation of rights or interests, or the imposition of liabilities or conditions, in relation to property transferred, or rights or interests acquired, by virtue of such legislation,

(b) provide for any property, liabilities or conditions to be determined under such legislation,

(c) make provision (other than provision imposing a charge to tax) as to the tax treatment of anything done by virtue of such legislation.

(3) No order shall be made by a Minister of the Crown by virtue of subsection (2)(c), and no recommendation shall be made to Her Majesty in Council to make an Order in Council by virtue of subsection (2)(c), without the agreement of the Treasury.

(4) Subordinate legislation to which this section applies shall have effect in relation to any property or liabilities to which it applies despite any provision (of whatever nature) which would otherwise prevent, penalise or restrict the transfer of the property or liabilities.

(5) A right of pre-emption, right of irritancy, right of return or other similar right shall not operate or become exercisable as a result of any transfer of property by virtue of any subordinate legislation to which this section applies.

(6) Any such right shall have effect in the case of any such transfer as if the transferee were the same person in law as the transferor and as if no transfer of the property had taken place.

(7) Such compensation as is just shall be paid to any person in respect of any such right which would, apart from subsection (5), have operated in favour of, or become exercisable by, that person but which, in consequence of the operation of that subsection, cannot subsequently operate in his favour or (as the case may be) become exercisable by him.

(8) Any compensation payable by virtue of subsection (7) shall be paid by the transferor or by the transferee or by both.

(9) Subordinate legislation under this subsection may provide for the determination of any disputes as to whether and, if so, how much, compensation is payable by virtue of subsection (7) and as to the person to whom or by whom it shall be paid.

(10) Subsections (4) to (9) apply in relation to the creation of rights or interests, or the doing of anything else, in relation to property as they apply in relation to a transfer of property; and references to the transferor and transferee shall be read accordingly.

(11) A certificate issued by the Secretary of State that any property or liability has, or has not, been transferred by virtue of subordinate legislation under section 60 or 62 or paragraph 2 of Schedule 2 shall be conclusive evidence of the transfer or (as the case may be) the fact that there has not been a transfer.

(12) A certificate issued by the Secretary of State and the Scottish Ministers that any property or liability has, or has not, been transferred by virtue of an Order in Council

under section 90 or 109 shall be conclusive evidence of the transfer or (as the case may be) the fact that there has not been a transfer.

(13) In this section "right of return" means any right under a provision for the return or reversion of property in specified circumstances.

General modification of enactments

117 Ministers of the Crown

So far as may be necessary for the purpose or in consequence of the exercise of a function by a member of the Scottish Executive within devolved competence, any pre-commencement enactment or prerogative instrument, and any other instrument or document, shall be read as if references to a Minister of the Crown (however described) were or included references to the Scottish Ministers.

118 Subordinate instruments

(1) Subsection (2) applies in relation to the exercise by a member of the Scottish Executive within devolved competence of a function to make, confirm or approve subordinate legislation.

(2) If a pre-commencement enactment makes provision—

- (a) for any instrument or the draft of any instrument made in the exercise of such a function to be laid before Parliament or either House of Parliament,
- (b) for the annulment or approval of any such instrument or draft by or in pursuance of a resolution of either or both Houses of Parliament, or
- (c) prohibiting the making of such an instrument without that approval,

the provision shall have effect, so far as it relates to the exercise of the function by a member of the Scottish Executive within devolved competence, as if any reference in it to Parliament or either House of Parliament were a reference to the Scottish Parliament.

(3) Where—

- (a) a function of making, confirming or approving subordinate legislation conferred by a pre-commencement enactment is exercisable by a Scottish public authority with mixed functions or no reserved functions, and
- (b) a pre-commencement enactment makes such provision in relation to the exercise of the function as is mentioned in subsection (2),

the provision shall have effect, so far as it relates to the exercise of the function by that authority, as if any reference in it to Parliament or either House of Parliament were a reference to the Scottish Parliament.

(4) Where—

- (a) a function of making, confirming or approving subordinate legislation conferred by a pre-commencement enactment is exercisable within devolved competence by a person other than a Minister of the Crown, a member of the Scottish Executive or a Scottish public authority with mixed functions or no reserved functions, and
- (b) a pre-commencement enactment makes such provision in relation to the exercise of the function as is mentioned in subsection (2),

the provision shall have effect, so far as it relates to the exercise of the function by that person within devolved competence, as if any reference in it to Parliament or either House of Parliament were a reference to the Scottish Parliament.

(5) If a pre-commencement enactment applies the Statutory Instruments Act 1946 as if a function of the kind mentioned in subsection (3) or (4) were exercisable by a Minister of the Crown, that Act shall apply, so far as the function is exercisable as mentioned in paragraph (a) of subsection (3) or (as the case may be) (4), as if the function were exercisable by the Scottish Ministers.

119 Consolidated Fund etc

(1) In this section "Scottish functions" means—

(a) functions of the Scottish Ministers, the First Minister or the Lord Advocate which are exercisable within devolved competence,

(b) functions of any Scottish public authority with mixed functions or no reserved functions.

(2) Subject to subsections (3) and (5), a provision of a pre-commencement enactment which—

(a) requires or authorises the payment of any sum out of the Consolidated Fund or money provided by Parliament, or

(b) requires or authorises the payment of any sum into the Consolidated Fund,

shall cease to have effect in relation to any Scottish functions.

(3) A provision of a pre-commencement enactment which—

(a) charges any sum on the Consolidated Fund,

(b) requires the payment of any sum out of the Consolidated Fund without further appropriation, or

(c) requires or authorises the payment of any sum into the Consolidated Fund by a person other than a Minister of the Crown,

shall have effect in relation to any Scottish functions as if it provided for the sum to be charged on the Scottish Consolidated Fund or required it to be paid out of that Fund without further approval or required or authorised it to be paid into that Fund (as the case may be).

(4) Subsections (2) and (3) do not apply to the words from the beginning of section 2(3) of the European Communities Act 1972 (general implementation of Treaties) to "such Community obligation".

(5) A provision of a pre-commencement enactment which authorises any sums to be applied as money provided by Parliament instead of being paid into the Consolidated Fund shall have effect in relation to any Scottish functions as if it authorised those sums to be applied as if they had been paid out of the Scottish Consolidated Fund in accordance with rules under section 65(1)(c) instead of being paid into that Fund.

(6) Where a power to lend money under a pre-commencement enactment is exercisable by the Scottish Ministers, subsection (7) applies to any sums which, for the purpose or as the result of the exercise of the power, would be required (apart from that subsection) —

(a) to be issued by the Treasury out of the National Loans Fund, or

(b) to be paid into that Fund.

(7) Those sums shall instead—

(a) be paid out of the Scottish Consolidated Fund without further approval, or

(b) be paid into that Fund,

(as the case may be).

120 Accounts and audit

A provision of a pre-commencement enactment which—

(a) requires any account to be examined, certified and reported on by, or to be open to the inspection of, the Comptroller and Auditor General, or

(b) requires him to have access to any other document for carrying out any such examination,

shall have effect in relation to any Scottish functions (within the meaning of section 119) as if the references to the Comptroller and Auditor General were to the Auditor General for Scotland.

121 Requirements to lay reports etc. before Parliament

(1) This section applies where—

(a) a pre-commencement enactment makes provision for any report to be laid before Parliament or either House of Parliament, and

(b) the report concerns Scottish functions.

(2) If the report only concerns Scottish functions, it shall be laid instead before the Scottish Parliament.

(3) In any other case, it shall be laid before the Scottish Parliament as well as before Parliament or (as the case may be) either House of Parliament.

(4) In this section—

"report" includes accounts and any statement,

"Scottish functions" has the same meaning as in section 119.

122 Crown land

(1) In any provision about the application of any pre-commencement enactment to Crown land—

(a) references to a Minister of the Crown or government department shall be read as including the Scottish Ministers and the Lord Advocate, and

(b) references to a Minister of the Crown or government department having the management of the land shall be read as including any member of the Scottish Executive having the management of the land.

(2) In this section, "Crown land" has the meaning given by section 242 of the Town and Country Planning (Scotland) Act 1997.

123 Stamp duty

In section 55 of the Finance Act 1987 (Crown exemption from stamp duty) references to a Minister of the Crown shall be read as including the Scottish Ministers, the Lord Advocate and the Parliamentary corporation.

124 Modification of sections 94 and 117 to 122

(1) Subordinate legislation may provide for any provision of sections 94 and 117 to 122 not to apply, or to apply with modifications, in such cases as the person making the legislation considers appropriate.

(2) Subordinate legislation made by Her Majesty in Council or a Minister of the Crown under this Act may, in connection with any other provision made by the legislation, also provide for any provision of sections 94 and 117 to 122 not to apply, or to apply with modifications.

Amendments and repeals

125 Amendments and repeals

(1) Schedule 8 (which makes modifications of enactments) shall have effect.

(2) The enactments mentioned in Schedule 9 are repealed to the extent specified in that Schedule.

Final provisions

126 Interpretation

(1) In this Act—

"body" includes unincorporated association,

"constituencies" and "regions", in relation to the Parliament, mean the constituencies and regions provided for by Schedule 1,

"constituency member" means a member of the Parliament for a constituency,

"the Convention rights" has the same meaning as in the Human Rights Act 1998,

"document" means anything in which information is recorded in any form (and references to producing a document are to be read accordingly),

"enactment" includes an Act of the Scottish Parliament, Northern Ireland legislation (within the meaning of the Northern Ireland Act 1998) and an enactment comprised in subordinate legislation, and includes an enactment comprised in, or in subordinate legislation under, an Act of Parliament, whenever passed or made,

"financial year" means a year ending with 31st March,

"functions" includes powers and duties, and "confer", in relation to functions, includes impose,

"government department" means any department of the Government of the United Kingdom,

"the Human Rights Convention" means—

(a) the Convention for the Protection of Human Rights and Fundamental Freedoms, agreed by the Council of Europe at Rome on 4th November 1950, and

(b) the Protocols to the Convention,

as they have effect for the time being in relation to the United Kingdom,

"Minister of the Crown" includes the Treasury,

"modify" includes amend or repeal,

"occupational pension scheme", "personal pension scheme" and "public service pension scheme" have the meanings given by section 1 of the Pension Schemes Act 1993, but as if the reference to employed earners in the definition of personal pension scheme were to any earners,

"the Parliament" means the Scottish Parliament,

"parliamentary", in relation to constituencies, elections and electors, is to be taken to refer to the Parliament of the United Kingdom,

"prerogative instrument" means an Order in Council, warrant, charter or other instrument made under the prerogative,

"the principal appointed day" means the day appointed by an order under section 130 which is designated by the order as the principal appointed day,

"proceedings", in relation to the Parliament, includes proceedings of any committee or sub-committee,

"property" includes rights and interests of any description,

"regional member" means a member of the Parliament for a region,

"Scotland" includes so much of the internal waters and territorial sea of the United Kingdom as are adjacent to Scotland,

"Scottish public authority" means any public body (except the Parliamentary corporation), public office or holder of such an office whose functions (in each case) are exercisable only in or as regards Scotland,

"the Scottish zone" means the sea within British fishery limits (that is, the limits set by or under section 1 of the Fishery Limits Act 1976) which is adjacent to Scotland,

"standing orders" means standing orders of the Parliament,

"subordinate legislation" has the same meaning as in the Interpretation Act 1978 and also includes an instrument made under an Act of the Scottish Parliament,

"tribunal" means any tribunal in which legal proceedings may be brought.

(2) Her Majesty may by Order in Council determine, or make provision for determining, for the purposes of this Act any boundary between waters which are to be treated as internal waters or territorial sea of the United Kingdom, or sea within British fishery limits, adjacent to Scotland and those which are not.

(3) For the purposes of this Act—

(a) the question whether any function of a body, government department, office or office-holder relates to reserved matters is to be determined by reference to the purpose for which the function is exercisable, having regard (among other things) to the likely effects in all the circumstances of any exercise of the function, but

(b) bodies to which paragraph 3 of Part III of Schedule 5 applies are to be treated as if all their functions were functions which relate to reserved matters.

(4) References in this Act to Scots private law are to the following areas of the civil law of Scotland—

(a) the general principles of private law (including private international law),

(b) the law of persons (including natural persons, legal persons and unincorporated bodies),

(c) the law of obligations (including obligations arising from contract, unilateral promise, delict, unjustified enrichment and negotiorum gestio),

(d) the law of property (including heritable and moveable property, trusts and succession), and

(e) the law of actions (including jurisdiction, remedies, evidence, procedure, diligence, recognition and enforcement of court orders, limitation of actions and arbitration),

and include references to judicial review of administrative action.

(5) References in this Act to Scots criminal law include criminal offences, jurisdiction, evidence, procedure and penalties and the treatment of offenders.

(6) References in this Act and in any other enactment to the Scottish Administration are to the office-holders in the Scottish Administration and the members of the staff of the Scottish Administration.

(7) For the purposes of this Act—

(a) references to office-holders in the Scottish Administration are to—

(i) members of the Scottish Executive and junior Scottish Ministers, and

(ii) the holders of offices in the Scottish Administration which are not ministerial offices, and

(b) references to members of the staff of the Scottish Administration are to the staff of the persons referred to in paragraph (a).

(8) For the purposes of this Act, the offices in the Scottish Administration which are not ministerial offices are—

(a) the Registrar General of Births, Deaths and Marriages for Scotland, the Keeper of the Registers of Scotland and the Keeper of the Records of Scotland, and

(b) any other office of a description specified in an Order in Council made by Her Majesty under this subsection.

(9) In this Act—

(a) all those rights, powers, liabilities, obligations and restrictions from time to time created or arising by or under the Community Treaties, and

(b) all those remedies and procedures from time to time provided for by or under the Community Treaties,

are referred to as "Community law".

(10) In this Act, "international obligations" means any international obligations of the United Kingdom other than obligations to observe and implement Community law or the Convention rights.

(11) In this Act, "by virtue of" includes "by" and "under".

127 Index of defined expressions

In this Act, the expressions listed in the left-hand column have the meaning given by, or are to be interpreted in accordance with, the provisions listed in the right-hand column.

Expression	*Provision of this Act*
Act of the Scottish Parliament	Section 28(1)
Advocate General	Section 32(4)
Auditor General for Scotland	Section 69
Body	Section 126(1)
By virtue of	Section 126(11)
Clerk, and Assistant Clerk	Section 20 and paragraph 3 of Schedule 2
Community law	Section 126(9)
Constituencies and constituency member	Section 126(1)
The Convention rights	Section 126(1)
Cross-border public authority	Section 88(5)
Devolved competence (in relation to the exercise of functions)	Section 54
Document	Section 126(1)
Enactment	Sections 113(6) and 126(1)
Financial year	Section 126(1)
Functions	Section 126(1)
Government department	Section 126(1)
The Human Rights Convention	Section 126(1)
International obligations	Section 126(10)
Judicial Committee	Section 32(4)
Legislative competence	Section 29
Member of the Scottish Executive	Section 44(1)
Members of the staff of the Scottish Administration	Section 126(7)
Minister of the Crown	Section 126(1)
Modify	Section 126(1)
Occupational pension scheme, personal pension scheme and public service pension scheme	Section 126(1)
Office-holders in the Scottish Administration	Section 126(7)
Offices in the Scottish Administration which are not ministerial offices	Section 126(8)
Open power	Section 112(3)
The Parliament	Section 126(1)

Expression	*Provision of this Act*
"parliamentary" (in relation to constituencies, elections and electors)	Section 126(1)
The Parliamentary corporation	Section 21(1)
Pre-commencement enactment	Section 53(3)
Prerogative instrument	Section 126(1)
Presiding Officer	Section 19
Principal appointed day	Section 126(1)
Proceedings	Section 126(1)
Property	Section 126(1)
Regional list (in relation to a party)	Section 5(4)
Regional returning officer	Section 12(6)
Regional vote	Section 6(2)
Regions and regional member	Section 126(1)
Registered political party	Section 5(9)
Reserved matters	Schedule 5
Retained functions (in relation to the Lord Advocate)	Section 52(6)
Scotland	Section 126(1) and (2)
Scots criminal law	Section 126(5)
Scots private law	Section 126(4)
Scottish Administration	Section 126(6)
Scottish Ministers	Section 44(2)
Scottish public authority	Section 126(1)
Scottish public authority with mixed functions or no reserved functions	Paragraphs 1 and 2 of Part III of Schedule 5
Scottish Seal	Section 2(6)
The Scottish zone	Section 126(1)
Staff of the Parliament	Paragraph 3 of Schedule 2
Standing orders	Section 126(1)
Subordinate legislation	Section 126(1)
Tribunal	Section 126(1)

128 Expenses

(1) There shall be paid out of money provided by Parliament—

(a) any expenditure incurred by a Minister of the Crown by virtue of this Act, and

(b) any increase attributable to this Act in the sums payable out of money so provided under any other enactment.

(2) There shall be paid into the Consolidated Fund any sums received by a Minister of the Crown by virtue of this Act which are not payable into the National Loans Fund.

129 Transitional provisions etc

(1) Subordinate legislation may make such provision as the person making the legislation considers necessary or expedient for transitory or transitional purposes in connection with the coming into force of any provision of this Act.

(2) If any of the following provisions come into force before the Human Rights Act 1998 has come into force (or come fully into force), the provision shall have effect until the time when that Act is fully in force as it will have effect after that time: sections 29(2)(d), 57(2) and (3), 100 and 126(1) and Schedule 6.

130 Commencement

(1) Sections 19 to 43, Parts II to V, sections 117 to 124 and section 125 (except so far as relating to paragraphs 10, 11, 19 and 23(1) and (6) of Schedule 8) shall come into force on such day as the Secretary of State may by order appoint.

(2) Different days may be appointed under this section for different purposes.

131 Extent

Section 25 extends only to Scotland.

132 Short title

This Act may be cited as the Scotland Act 1998.

SCHEDULES

SCHEDULE 1

Section 1.

CONSTITUENCIES, REGIONS AND REGIONAL MEMBERS

General

1 The constituencies for the purposes of this Act are—

(a) the Orkney Islands,

(b) the Shetland Islands, and

(c) the parliamentary constituencies in Scotland, except a parliamentary constituency including either of those islands.

2 (1) There shall be eight regions for the purposes of this Act.

(2) Those regions shall be the eight European Parliamentary constituencies which were provided for by the European Parliamentary Constituencies (Scotland) Order 1996.

(3) Seven regional members shall be returned for each region.

(4) Sub-paragraphs (2) and (3) are subject to any Order in Council under the Parliamentary Constituencies Act 1986 (referred to in this Schedule as the 1986 Act), as that Act is extended by this Schedule.

Reports of Boundary Commission

3 (1) This paragraph applies where the Boundary Commission for Scotland (referred to in this Schedule as the Commission) submit a report to the Secretary of State under section 3(1) or (3) of the 1986 Act recommending any alteration in any parliamentary constituencies.

(2) In the report the Commission shall recommend any alteration—

(a) in any of the regions, or

(b) in the number of regional members to be returned for any of the regions,

which, in their opinion, is required to be made in order to give effect to the rules in paragraph 7.

(3) If in the case of a report under section 3(1) or (3) of that Act the Commission do not make any recommendation within sub-paragraph (2), they shall in the report state that, in their opinion, no such alteration is required.

(4) A report making a recommendation for an alteration in any region shall state—

(a) the name by which the Commission recommend that the region should be known, and

(b) the number of regional members to be returned for the region.

(5) The Commission shall lay any report recommending any alteration in parliamentary constituencies before the Parliament.

4 (1) An Order in Council under section 4 of the 1986 Act which has the effect of making any alteration in any constituency of the Parliament, or makes any alteration within paragraph 3(2), may come into force for the purposes of any election for membership of the Parliament on a different day from the day on which it comes into force for the purposes of any parliamentary election; and paragraph 1(c) shall be read accordingly.

(2) The coming into force of such an Order, so far as it has the effect of making any alteration in any constituency of the Parliament or makes any alteration within paragraph 3(2), shall not affect the return of any member of the Parliament, or its constitution, until the Parliament is dissolved.

Notices

5 (1) Where the Commission have provisionally determined to make recommendations affecting any region, they shall publish in at least one newspaper circulating in the region a notice stating—

(a) the effect of the proposed recommendations and (except in a case where they propose to recommend that no alteration within paragraph 3(2) be made) that a copy of the recommendations is open to inspection at a specified place or places within the region, and

(b) that representations with respect to the proposed recommendations may be made to the Commission within one month after the publication of the notice;

and the Commission shall take into consideration any representations duly made in accordance with any such notice.

(2) Where the Commission revise any proposed recommendations after publishing notice of them under sub-paragraph (1), the Commission shall comply again with that sub-paragraph in relation to the revised recommendations, as if no earlier notice had been published.

Local inquiries

6 (1) The Commission may, if they think fit, cause a local inquiry to be held in respect of any region.

(2) If, on the publication of a notice under paragraph 5(1) of a recommendation for any alteration within paragraph 3(2), the Commission receive any representation objecting to the proposed recommendation—

(a) from an interested authority, or

(b) from a body of electors numbering 500 or more,

the Commission shall not make the recommendation unless a local inquiry has been held in respect of the region since the publication of the notice.

(3) If a local inquiry was held in respect of the region before the publication of the notice under paragraph 5(1), sub-paragraph (2) shall not apply if the Commission, after considering the matters discussed at the local inquiry, the nature of the representations received on the publication of the notice and any other relevant circumstances, are of the opinion that a further local inquiry would not be justified.

(4) In this paragraph, in relation to any recommendation—

"interested authority" means the council for an area which is wholly or partly included in the region affected by the recommendation, and "elector" means an elector for the purposes of an election for membership of the Parliament in any constituency included in the region.

(5) Sections 210(4) and (5) of the Local Government (Scotland) Act 1973 (attendance of witnesses at inquiries) shall apply in relation to any local inquiry held under this paragraph.

The rules

7 (1) The rules referred to in paragraph 3 are:

1 A constituency shall fall wholly within a region.

2 The regional electorate of any region shall be as near the regional electorate of each of the other regions as is reasonably practicable having regard, where appropriate, to special geographical considerations.

3 So far as reasonably practicable, the ratio which the number of regional member seats bears to the number of constituency member seats shall be 56 to 73.

4 The number of regional member seats for a region shall be—

(a) one eighth of the total number of regional member seats, or

(b) (if that total number is not exactly divisible by eight) either one eighth of the highest number which is less than that total number and exactly divisible by eight or the number produced by adding one to one eighth of that highest number (as provided by sub-paragraphs (2) to (4)).

(2) If the total number of regional member seats is not exactly divisible by eight, the Commission shall calculate the difference between—

(a) the total number of regional member seats, and

(b) the highest number which is less than that total number and exactly divisible by eight,

and that is the number of residual seats to be allocated by the Commission.

(3) The Commission shall not allocate more than one residual seat for a region.

(4) The Commission shall divide the regional electorate for each region by the aggregate of—

(a) the number of constituencies in the region, and

(b) one eighth of the highest number which is less than the total number of regional member seats and exactly divisible by eight,

and, in allocating the residual seat or seats for a region or regions, shall have regard to the desirability of allocating the residual seat or seats to the region or regions for which that calculation produces the highest number or numbers.

8 (1) For the purposes of any report of the Commission in relation to a region, the regional electorate is the number of persons—

(a) whose names appear on the enumeration date on the registers of local government electors, and

(b) who are registered at addresses within a constituency included in the region.

(2) In sub-paragraph (1), "the enumeration date" means the date on which the notice about the report is published in accordance with section 5(1) of the 1986 Act.

SCHEDULE 2

Section 21.

SCOTTISH PARLIAMENTARY CORPORATE BODY

Membership

1 A person appointed under section 21(2)(b) shall hold office until another member of the Parliament is appointed in his place unless he previously resigns, ceases to be a member of the Parliament otherwise than by virtue of a dissolution or is removed from office by resolution of the Parliament.

Property

2 (1) The corporation may hold property.

(2) Subordinate legislation may provide—

(a) for the transfer to the corporation of any property belonging to a Minister of the Crown or government department, or

(b) for the corporation to have such rights or interests in relation to any property belonging to a Minister of the Crown or government department as the person making the legislation considers appropriate (whether in connection with a transfer or otherwise).

(3) Subordinate legislation under sub-paragraph (2) in relation to any property may provide for the transfer to the corporation of any liabilities relating to the property to which a Minister of the Crown or government department is subject and which subsist immediately before the subordinate legislation comes into force.

(4) Subordinate legislation under sub-paragraph (2) may only be made if the person making the legislation considers it appropriate to do so to enable the corporation to exercise its functions or to facilitate their exercise or in connection with their exercise or proposed exercise.

Staff

3 (1) The corporation shall appoint Assistant Clerks and may appoint other staff.

(2) The Clerk and other persons appointed by the corporation are referred to in this Act as the staff of the Parliament.

(3) It is for the corporation to determine the terms and conditions of appointment of the staff of the Parliament, including arrangements for the payment of pensions, gratuities or allowances to, or in respect of, any person who has ceased to be a member of the staff of the Parliament.

(4) In particular, the corporation may—

(a) make contributions or payments towards provision for such pensions, gratuities or allowances,

(b) establish and administer one or more pension schemes.

Powers

4 (1) Subject to sub-paragraph (4), the corporation may do anything which appears to it to be necessary or expedient for the purpose of or in connection with the discharge of its functions.

(2) That includes, in particular—

(a) entering into contracts,

(b) charging for goods or services,

(c) investing sums not immediately required in relation to the discharge of its functions, and

(d) accepting gifts.

(3) The corporation may sell goods or provide services, and may make arrangements for the sale of goods or provision of services, to the public.

(4) The corporation may borrow sums in sterling by way of overdraft or otherwise for the purpose of meeting a temporary excess of expenditure over sums otherwise available to meet that expenditure.

(5) The corporation may borrow money only under sub-paragraph (4) and may borrow under that sub-paragraph only in accordance with the special or general approval of the Parliament.

Delegation

5 The corporation may delegate any of its functions to the Presiding Officer or the Clerk.

Proceedings and business

6 (1) The validity of any act of the corporation shall not be affected by any vacancy among the members, or by any defect in the appointment, or qualification for membership, of any member.

(2) The corporation may determine its own procedure.

(3) The Presiding Officer shall preside at meetings of the corporation, but the corporation may appoint another of its members to preside if the office of Presiding Officer is vacant or the Presiding Officer is for any reason unable to act.

Crown status

7 (1) Her Majesty may by Order in Council provide for the corporation to be treated to any extent as a Crown body for the purposes of any enactment.

(2) In particular, the Order may for the purposes of any enactment provide—

(a) for employment under the corporation to be treated as employment under the corporation as a Crown body,

(b) for land held, used or managed by the corporation, or operations carried out by or on behalf of the corporation, to be treated (as the case may be) as land held, used or managed, or operations carried out by or on behalf of, the corporation as a Crown body.

(3) For the purposes of this paragraph, "Crown body" means a body which is the servant or agent of the Crown, and includes a government department.

SCHEDULE 3

Section 22.

STANDING ORDERS – FURTHER PROVISION

Preservation of order

1 (1) The standing orders shall include provision for preserving order in the proceedings of the Parliament, including provision for—

(a) preventing conduct which would constitute a criminal offence or contempt of court, and

(b) a sub judice rule.

(2) Such provision may provide for excluding a member of the Parliament from proceedings.

Withdrawal of rights and privileges

2 The standing orders may include provision for withdrawing from a member of the Parliament his rights and privileges as a member.

Proceedings to be in public

3 (1) The standing orders shall include provision requiring the proceedings of the Parliament to be held in public, except in such circumstances as the standing orders may provide.

(2) The standing orders may include provision as to the conditions to be complied with by any member of the public attending the proceedings, including provision for excluding from the proceedings any member of the public who does not comply with those conditions.

Reporting and publishing proceedings

4 The standing orders shall include provision for reporting the proceedings of the Parliament and for publishing the reports.

The Presiding Officer and deputies

5 The standing orders shall include provision for ensuring that the Presiding Officer and deputies do not all represent the same political party.

Committees

6 (1) Standing orders which provide for the appointment of committees may include provision for those committees to have power to appoint sub-committees.

(2) The standing orders shall include provision for ensuring that, in appointing members to committees and sub-committees, regard is had to the balance of political parties in the Parliament.

(3) The standing orders may include provision for excluding from the proceedings of a committee or sub-committee a member of the Parliament who is not a member of the committee or sub-committee.

Crown interests

7 The standing orders shall include provision for ensuring that a Bill containing provisions which would, if the Bill were a Bill for an Act of Parliament, require the consent of Her Majesty, the Prince and Steward of Scotland or the Duke of Cornwall shall not pass unless such consent has been signified to the Parliament.

SCHEDULE 4

Sections 29 and 53(4).

ENACTMENTS ETC. PROTECTED FROM MODIFICATION

PART I

THE PROTECTED PROVISIONS

Particular enactments

1 (1) An Act of the Scottish Parliament cannot modify, or confer power by subordinate legislation to modify, any of the following provisions.

(2) The provisions are—

(a) Articles 4 and 6 of the Union with Scotland Act 1706 and of the Union with England Act 1707 so far as they relate to freedom of trade,

(b) the Private Legislation Procedure (Scotland) Act 1936,

(c) the following provisions of the European Communities Act 1972—

Section 1 and Schedule 1,

Section 2, other than subsection (2), the words following "such Community obligation" in subsection (3) and the words "subject to Schedule 2 to this Act" in subsection (4),

Section 3(1) and (2),

Section 11(2),

(d) paragraphs 5(3)(b) and 15(4)(b) of Schedule 32 to the Local Government, Planning and Land Act 1980 (designation of enterprise zones),

(e) sections 140A to 140G of the Social Security Administration Act 1992 (rent rebate and rent allowance subsidy and council tax benefit),

(f) the Human Rights Act 1998.

The law on reserved matters

2 (1) An Act of the Scottish Parliament cannot modify, or confer power by subordinate legislation to modify, the law on reserved matters.

(2) In this paragraph, "the law on reserved matters" means—

(a) any enactment the subject-matter of which is a reserved matter and which is comprised in an Act of Parliament or subordinate legislation under an Act of Parliament, and

(b) any rule of law which is not contained in an enactment and the subject-matter of which is a reserved matter,

and in this sub-paragraph "Act of Parliament" does not include this Act.

(3) Sub-paragraph (1) applies in relation to a rule of Scots private law or Scots criminal law (whether or not contained in an enactment) only to the extent that the rule in question is special to a reserved matter or the subject-matter of the rule is—

(a) interest on sums due in respect of taxes or excise duties and refunds of such taxes or duties, or

(b) the obligations, in relation to occupational or personal pension schemes, of the trustees or managers.

(4) Sub-paragraph (3)(b) extends to cases where liabilities under orders made in matrimonial proceedings, or agreements made between the parties to a marriage, are to be satisfied out of assets of the scheme.

3 (1) Paragraph 2 does not apply to modifications which—

(a) are incidental to, or consequential on, provision made (whether by virtue of the Act in question or another enactment) which does not relate to reserved matters, and

(b) do not have a greater effect on reserved matters than is necessary to give effect to the purpose of the provision.

(2) In determining for the purposes of sub-paragraph (1)(b) what is necessary to give effect to the purpose of a provision, any power to make laws other than the power of the Parliament is to be disregarded.

This Act

4 (1) An Act of the Scottish Parliament cannot modify, or confer power by subordinate legislation to modify, this Act.

(2) This paragraph does not apply to modifying sections 1(4), 17(5), 19(7), 21(5), 24(2), 28(5), 39(7), 40 to 43, 50, 69(3), 85 and 93 and paragraphs 4(1) to (3) and 6(1) of Schedule 2.

(3) This paragraph does not apply to modifying any provision of this Act (other than sections 64(7), 66(2), 71(7), 77, 78 and 119) which—

(a) charges any sum on the Scottish Consolidated Fund,

(b) requires any sum to be paid out of that Fund without further approval, or

(c) requires or authorises the payment of any sum into that Fund.

(4) This paragraph does not apply to any modifications of Part III which are necessary or expedient for the purpose or in consequence of the establishment of a new fund,

in addition to the Scottish Consolidated Fund, out of which loans may be made by the Scottish Ministers.

(5) This paragraph does not apply to—

(a) modifying so much of any enactment as is modified by this Act,

(b) repealing so much of any provision of this Act as amends any enactment, if the provision ceases to have effect in consequence of any enactment comprised in or made under an Act of the Scottish Parliament.

Enactments modified by this Act

5 An Act of the Scottish Parliament cannot modify, or confer power by subordinate legislation to modify—

(a) the effect of section 119(3) in relation to any provision of an Act of Parliament relating to judicial salaries,

(b) so much of any enactment as—

(i) is amended by paragraph 2, 7 or 32 of Schedule 8, and

(ii) relates to the Advocate General,

(c) so much of any enactment as is amended by paragraph 9(b) or 29 of Schedule 8.

Shared powers

6 An Act of the Scottish Parliament cannot modify, or confer power by subordinate legislation to modify, any enactment so far as the enactment relates to powers exercisable by a Minister of the Crown by virtue of section 56.

PART II

GENERAL EXCEPTIONS

Restatement, etc.

7 (1) Part I of this Schedule does not prevent an Act of the Scottish Parliament—

(a) restating the law (or restating it with such modifications as are not prevented by that Part), or

(b) repealing any spent enactment,

or conferring power by subordinate legislation to do so.

(2) For the purposes of paragraph 2, the law on reserved matters includes any restatement in an Act of the Scottish Parliament, or subordinate legislation under such an Act, of the law on reserved matters if the subject-matter of the restatement is a reserved matter.

Effect of Interpretation Act 1978

8 Part I of this Schedule does not prevent the operation of any provision of the Interpretation Act 1978.

Change of title etc.

9 (1) Part I of this Schedule does not prevent an Act of the Scottish Parliament amending, or conferring power by subordinate legislation to amend, any enactment by changing—

(a) any of the titles referred to in sub-paragraph (2), or

(b) any reference to a declarator,

in consequence of any provision made by or under an Act of the Scottish Parliament.

(2) The titles are those of—

(a) any court or tribunal or any judge, chairman or officer of a court or tribunal,

(b) any holder of an office in the Scottish Administration which is not a ministerial office or any member of the staff of the Scottish Administration,

(c) any register.

Accounts and audit and maladministration

10 Part I of this Schedule does not prevent an Act of the Scottish Parliament modifying, or conferring power by subordinate legislation to modify, any enactment for or in connection with the purposes of section 70 or 91.

Subordinate legislation

11 (1) Part I of this Schedule does not prevent an Act of the Scottish Parliament modifying, or conferring power by subordinate legislation to modify, any enactment for or in connection with any of the following purposes.

(2) Those purposes are—

(a) making different provision in respect of the document by which a power to make subordinate legislation within sub-paragraph (3) is to be exercised,

(b) making different provision (or no provision) for the procedure, in relation to the Parliament, to which legislation made in the exercise of such a power (or the instrument or other document in which it is contained) is to be subject,

(c) applying any enactment comprised in or made under an Act of the Scottish Parliament relating to the documents by which such powers may be exercised.

(3) The power to make the subordinate legislation, or a power to confirm or approve the legislation, must be exercisable by—

(a) a member of the Scottish Executive,

(b) any Scottish public authority with mixed functions or no reserved functions,

(c) any other person (not being a Minister of the Crown) within devolved competence.

PART III

CONSEQUENTIAL MODIFICATION OF SECTIONS 53 AND 54

12 (1) This paragraph applies to a function which (apart from this Schedule) would be transferred to the Scottish Ministers by virtue of section 53(2)(c).

(2) If, because of anything in Part I of this Schedule, a provision of an Act of the Scottish Parliament modifying an enactment so as to provide for the function to be exercisable by a different person would be outside the legislative competence of the Parliament, the function is not so transferred.

13 (1) Paragraph 12 does not apply to any function conferred by any provision of—

(a) the European Communities Act 1972,

(b) the Human Rights Act 1998, except sections 1, 5, 14 to 17 and 22 of that Act,

(c) the law on reserved matters (for the purposes of paragraph 2) so far as contained in an enactment.

(2) For the purpose of determining—

(a) whether any function under any of the provisions referred to in sub-paragraph (1) is transferred to the Scottish Ministers by virtue of section 53, and

(b) the extent to which any such function (other than a function of making, confirming or approving subordinate legislation) is exercisable by them,

the references in section 54 to the legislative competence of the Parliament are to be read as if section 29(2)(c) were omitted.

(3) Part I of this Schedule does not prevent an Act of the Scottish Parliament modifying, or conferring power by subordinate legislation to modify, any of the provisions mentioned in sub-paragraph (1) so as to provide for a function transferred to the Scottish Ministers by virtue of section 53 to be exercisable by a different person.

14 If any pre-commencement enactment or prerogative instrument is modified by subordinate legislation under section 105, a function under that enactment or instrument (whether as it has effect before or after the modification) is not transferred by virtue of section 53 if the subordinate legislation provides that it is not to be so transferred.

SCHEDULE 5

Section 30.

Reserved Matters

Part I

General reservations

The Constitution

1 The following aspects of the constitution are reserved matters, that is—

(a) the Crown, including succession to the Crown and a regency,

(b) the Union of the Kingdoms of Scotland and England,

(c) the Parliament of the United Kingdom,

(d) the continued existence of the High Court of Justiciary as a criminal court of first instance and of appeal,

(e) the continued existence of the Court of Session as a civil court of first instance and of appeal.

2 (1) Paragraph 1 does not reserve—

(a) Her Majesty's prerogative and other executive functions,

(b) functions exercisable by any person acting on behalf of the Crown, or

(c) any office in the Scottish Administration.

(2) Sub-paragraph (1) does not affect the reservation by paragraph 1 of honours and dignities or the functions of the Lord Lyon King of Arms so far as relating to the granting of arms; but this sub-paragraph does not apply to the Lord Lyon King of Arms in his judicial capacity.

(3) Sub-paragraph (1) does not affect the reservation by paragraph 1 of the management (in accordance with any enactment regulating the use of land) of the Crown Estate.

(4) Sub-paragraph (1) does not affect the reservation by paragraph 1 of the functions of the Security Service, the Secret Intelligence Service and the Government Communications Headquarters.

3 (1) Paragraph 1 does not reserve property belonging to Her Majesty in right of the Crown or belonging to any person acting on behalf of the Crown or held in trust for Her Majesty for the purposes of any person acting on behalf of the Crown.

(2) Paragraph 1 does not reserve the ultimate superiority of the Crown or the superiority of the Prince and Steward of Scotland.

(3) Sub-paragraph (1) does not affect the reservation by paragraph 1 of—

(a) the hereditary revenues of the Crown, other than revenues from bona vacantia, ultimus haeres and treasure trove,

(b) the royal arms and standard,

(c) the compulsory acquisition of property held or used by a Minister of the Crown or government department.

4 (1) Paragraph 1 does not reserve property held by Her Majesty in Her private capacity.

(2) Sub-paragraph (1) does not affect the reservation by paragraph 1 of the subject-matter of the Crown Private Estates Acts 1800 to 1873.

5 Paragraph 1 does not reserve the use of the Scottish Seal.

Political parties

6 The registration and funding of political parties is a reserved matter.

Foreign affairs etc.

7 (1) International relations, including relations with territories outside the United Kingdom, the European Communities (and their institutions) and other international organisations, regulation of international trade, and international development assistance and co-operation are reserved matters.

(2) Sub-paragraph (1) does not reserve—

(a) observing and implementing international obligations, obligations under the Human Rights Convention and obligations under Community law,

(b) assisting Ministers of the Crown in relation to any matter to which that sub-paragraph applies.

Public service

8 (1) The Civil Service of the State is a reserved matter.

(2) Sub-paragraph (1) does not reserve the subject-matter of—

(a) Part I of the Sheriff Courts and Legal Officers (Scotland) Act 1927 (appointment of sheriff clerks and procurators fiscal etc.),

(b) Part III of the Administration of Justice (Scotland) Act 1933 (officers of the High Court of Justiciary and of the Court of Session).

Defence

9 (1) The following are reserved matters—

(a) the defence of the realm,

(b) the naval, military or air forces of the Crown, including reserve forces,

(c) visiting forces,

(d) international headquarters and defence organisations,

(e) trading with the enemy and enemy property.

(2) Sub-paragraph (1) does not reserve—

(a) the exercise of civil defence functions by any person otherwise than as a member of any force or organisation referred to in sub-paragraph (1)(b) to (d) or any other force or organisation reserved by virtue of sub-paragraph (1)(a),

(b) the conferral of enforcement powers in relation to sea fishing.

Treason

10 Treason (including constructive treason), treason felony and misprision of treason are reserved matters.

PART II

SPECIFIC RESERVATIONS

Preliminary

1 The matters to which any of the Sections in this Part apply are reserved matters for the purposes of this Act.

2 A Section applies to any matter described or referred to in it when read with any illustrations, exceptions or interpretation provisions in that Section.

3 Any illustrations, exceptions or interpretation provisions in a Section relate only to that Section (so that an entry under the heading "exceptions" does not affect any other Section).

Reservations

Head A – Financial and Economic Matters

A1. Fiscal, economic and monetary policy

Fiscal, economic and monetary policy, including the issue and circulation of money, taxes and excise duties, government borrowing and lending, control over United Kingdom public expenditure, the exchange rate and the Bank of England.

Exception

Local taxes to fund local authority expenditure (for example, council tax and non-domestic rates).

A2. The currency

Coinage, legal tender and bank notes.

A3. Financial services

Financial services, including investment business, banking and deposit-taking, collective investment schemes and insurance.

Exception

The subject-matter of section 1 of the Banking and Financial Dealings Act 1971 (bank holidays).

A4. Financial markets

Financial markets, including listing and public offers of securities and investments, transfer of securities and insider dealing.

A5. Money laundering

The subject-matter of the Money Laundering Regulations 1993, but in relation to any type of business.

Head B – Home Affairs

B1. Misuse of drugs

The subject-matter of—

(a) the Misuse of Drugs Act 1971,

(b) sections 12 to 14 of the Criminal Justice (International Co-operation) Act 1990 (substances useful for manufacture of controlled drugs), and

(c) Part V of the Criminal Law (Consolidation) (Scotland) Act 1995 (drug trafficking) and, so far as relating to drug trafficking, the Proceeds of Crime (Scotland) Act 1995.

B2. Data protection

The subject-matter of—

(a) the Data Protection Act 1998, and

(b) Council Directive 95/46/EC (protection of individuals with regard to the processing of personal data and on the free movement of such data).

Interpretation

If any provision of the Data Protection Act 1998 is not in force on the principal appointed day, it is to be treated for the purposes of this reservation as if it were.

B3. Elections

Elections for membership of the House of Commons, the European Parliament and the Parliament, including the subject-matter of—

(a) the European Parliamentary Elections Act 1978,

(b) the Representation of the People Act 1983 and the Representation of the People Act 1985, and

(c) the Parliamentary Constituencies Act 1986,

so far as those enactments apply, or may be applied, in respect of such membership.

The franchise at local government elections.

B4. Firearms

The subject-matter of the Firearms Acts 1968 to 1997.

B5. Entertainment

The subject-matter of—

(a) the Video Recordings Act 1984, and

(b) sections 1 to 3 and 5 to 16 of the Cinemas Act 1985 (control of exhibitions).

The classification of films for public exhibition by reference to their suitability for viewing by persons generally or above a particular age, with or without any advice as to the desirability of parental guidance.

B6. Immigration and nationality

Nationality; immigration, including asylum and the status and capacity of persons in the United Kingdom who are not British citizens; free movement of persons within the European Economic Area; issue of travel documents.

B7.Scientific procedures on live animals

The subject-matter of the Animals (Scientific Procedures) Act 1986.

B8. National security, interception of communications, official secrets and terrorism

National security.

The interception of communications; but not the subject-matter of Part III of the Police Act 1997 (authorisation to interfere with property etc.) or surveillance not involving interference with property.

The subject-matter of—

(a) the Official Secrets Acts 1911 and 1920, and

(b) the Official Secrets Act 1989, except so far as relating to any information, document or other article protected against disclosure by section 4(2) (crime) and not by any other provision of sections 1 to 4.

Special powers, and other special provisions, for dealing with terrorism.

B9. Betting, gaming and lotteries

Betting, gaming and lotteries.

B10. Emergency powers

Emergency powers.

B11. Extradition

Extradition.

B12. Lieutenancies

The subject-matter of the Lieutenancies Act 1997.

Head C – Trade and Industry

C1. Business associations

The creation, operation, regulation and dissolution of types of business association.

Exceptions

The creation, operation, regulation and dissolution of—

(a) particular public bodies, or public bodies of a particular type, established by or under any enactment, and

(b) charities.

Interpretation

"Business association" means any person (other than an individual) established for the purpose of carrying on any kind of business, whether or not for profit; and "business" includes the provision of benefits to the members of an association.

C2. Insolvency

In relation to business associations—

(a) the modes of, the grounds for and the general legal effect of winding up, and the persons who may initiate winding up,

(b) liability to contribute to assets on winding up,

(c) powers of courts in relation to proceedings for winding up, other than the power to sist proceedings,

(d) arrangements with creditors, and

(e) procedures giving protection from creditors.

Preferred or preferential debts for the purposes of the Bankruptcy (Scotland) Act 1985, the Insolvency Act 1986, and any other enactment relating to the sequestration of the estate of any person or to the winding up of business associations, the preference of such debts against other such debts and the extent of their preference over other types of debt.

Regulation of insolvency practitioners.

Co-operation of insolvency courts.

Exceptions

In relation to business associations—

(a) the process of winding up, including the person having responsibility for the conduct of a winding up or any part of it, and his conduct of it or of that part,

(b) the effect of winding up on diligence, and

(c) avoidance and adjustment of prior transactions on winding up.

Floating charges and receivers, except in relation to preferential debts, regulation of insolvency practitioners and co-operation of insolvency courts.

Interpretation

"Business association" has the meaning given in Section C1 of this Part of this Schedule, but does not include any person whose estate may be sequestrated under the Bankruptcy (Scotland) Act 1985 or any public body established by or under an enactment.

"Winding up", in relation to business associations, includes winding up of solvent, as well as insolvent, business associations.

C3. Competition

Regulation of anti-competitive practices and agreements; abuse of dominant position; monopolies and mergers.

Exception

Regulation of particular practices in the legal profession for the purpose of regulating that profession or the provision of legal services.

Interpretation

"The legal profession" means advocates, solicitors and qualified conveyancers and executry practitioners within the meaning of Part II of the Law Reform (Miscellaneous Provisions) (Scotland) Act 1990.

C4. Intellectual property

Intellectual property.

Exception

The subject-matter of Parts I and II of the Plant Varieties Act 1997 (plant varieties and the Plant Varieties and Seeds Tribunal).

C5. Import and export control

The subject-matter of the Import, Export and Customs Powers (Defence) Act 1939.

Prohibition and regulation of the import and export of endangered species of animals and plants.

Exceptions

Prohibition and regulation of movement into and out of Scotland of—

(a) food, animals, animal products, plants and plant products for the purposes of protecting human, animal or plant health, animal welfare or the environment or observing or implementing obligations under the Common Agricultural Policy, and

(b) animal feeding stuffs, fertilisers and pesticides for the purposes of protecting human, animal or plant health or the environment.

C6. Sea fishing

Regulation of sea fishing outside the Scottish zone (except in relation to Scottish fishing boats).

Interpretation

"Scottish fishing boat" means a fishing vessel which is registered in the register maintained under section 8 of the Merchant Shipping Act 1995 and whose entry in the register specifies a port in Scotland as the port to which the vessel is to be treated as belonging.

C7. Consumer protection

Regulation of—

(a) the sale and supply of goods and services to consumers,

(b) guarantees in relation to such goods and services,

(c) hire-purchase, including the subject-matter of Part III of the Hire-Purchase Act 1964,

(d) trade descriptions, except in relation to food,

(e) misleading and comparative advertising, except regulation specifically in relation to food, tobacco and tobacco products,

(f) price indications,

(g) trading stamps,

(h) auctions and mock auctions of goods and services, and
(i) hallmarking and gun barrel proofing.

Safety of, and liability for, services supplied to consumers.

The subject-matter of—
(a) the Hearing Aid Council Act 1968,
(b) the Unsolicited Goods and Services Acts 1971 and 1975,
(c) Parts I to III and XI of the Fair Trading Act 1973,
(d) the Consumer Credit Act 1974,
(e) the Estate Agents Act 1979,
(f) the Timeshare Act 1992,
(g) the Package Travel, Package Holidays and Package Tours Regulations 1992, and
(h) the Commercial Agents (Council Directive) Regulations 1993.

Exception

The subject-matter of section 16 of the Food Safety Act 1990 (food safety and consumer protection).

C8. Product standards, safety and liability

Technical standards and requirements in relation to products in pursuance of an obligation under Community law.

Product safety and liability.

Product labelling.

Exceptions

Food, agricultural and horticultural produce, fish and fish products, seeds, animal feeding stuffs, fertilisers and pesticides.

In relation to food safety, materials which come into contact with food.

C9. Weights and measures

Units and standards of weight and measurement.

Regulation of trade so far as involving weighing, measuring and quantities.

C10. Telecommunications and wireless telegraphy

Telecommunications and wireless telegraphy.

Internet services.

Electronic encryption.

The subject-matter of Part II of the Wireless Telegraphy Act 1949 (electromagnetic disturbance).

Exception

The subject-matter of Part III of the Police Act 1997 (authorisation to interfere with property etc.).

C11. Post Office, posts and postal services

The Post Office, posts (including postage stamps, postal orders and postal packets) and regulation of postal services.

C12. Research Councils

Research Councils within the meaning of the Science and Technology Act 1965.

The subject-matter of section 5 of that Act (funding of scientific research) so far as relating to Research Councils.

C13. Designation of assisted areas

The subject-matter of section 1 of the Industrial Development Act 1982.

C14. Industrial Development Advisory Board

The Industrial Development Advisory Board.

C15. Protection of trading and economic interests

The subject-matter of—

(a) section 2 of the Emergency Laws (Re-enactments and Repeals) Act 1964 (Treasury power in relation to action damaging to economic position of United Kingdom),

(b) Part II of the Industry Act 1975 (powers in relation to transfer of control of important manufacturing undertakings), and

(c) the Protection of Trading Interests Act 1980.

Head D – Energy

D1. Electricity

Generation, transmission, distribution and supply of electricity.

The subject-matter of Part II of the Electricity Act 1989.

Exception

The subject-matter of Part I of the Environmental Protection Act 1990.

D2. Oil and gas

Oil and gas, including—

(a) the ownership of, exploration for and exploitation of deposits of oil and natural gas,

(b) the subject-matter of section 1 of the Mineral Exploration and Investment Grants Act 1972 (contributions in connection with mineral exploration) so far as relating to exploration for oil and gas,

(c) offshore installations and pipelines,

(d) the subject-matter of the Pipe-lines Act 1962 (including section 5 (deemed planning permission)) so far as relating to pipelines within the meaning of section 65 of that Act,

(e) the application of Scots law and the jurisdiction of the Scottish courts in relation to offshore activities,

(f) pollution relating to oil and gas exploration and exploitation, but only outside controlled waters (within the meaning of section 30A(1) of the Control of Pollution Act 1974),

(g) the subject-matter of Part II of the Food and Environment Protection Act 1985 so far as relating to oil and gas exploration and exploitation, but only in relation to activities outside such controlled waters,

(h) restrictions on navigation, fishing and other activities in connection with offshore activities,
(i) liquefaction of natural gas, and
(j) the conveyance, shipping and supply of gas through pipes.

Exceptions

The subject-matter of—
(a) sections 10 to 12 of the Industry Act 1972 (credits and grants for construction of ships and offshore installations),
(b) the Offshore Petroleum Development (Scotland) Act 1975, other than sections 3 to 7, and
(c) Part I of the Environmental Protection Act 1990.

The manufacture of gas.

The conveyance, shipping and supply of gas other than through pipes.

D3. Coal

Coal, including its ownership and exploitation, deep and opencast coal mining and coal mining subsidence.

Exceptions

The subject-matter of—
(a) Part I of the Environmental Protection Act 1990, and
(b) sections 53 (environmental duties in connection with planning) and 54 (obligation to restore land affected by coal-mining operations) of the Coal Industry Act 1994.

D4. Nuclear energy

Nuclear energy and nuclear installations, including—
(a) nuclear safety, security and safeguards, and
(b) liability for nuclear occurrences.

Exceptions

The subject-matter of—
(a) Part I of the Environmental Protection Act 1990, and
(b) the Radioactive Substances Act 1993.

D5. Energy conservation

The subject-matter of the Energy Act 1976, other than section 9.

Exception

The encouragement of energy efficiency other than by prohibition or regulation.

Head E – Transport

E1. Road transport

The subject-matter of—
(a) the Motor Vehicles (International Circulation) Act 1952,
(b) the Public Passenger Vehicles Act 1981 and the Transport Act 1985, so far as relating to public service vehicle operator licensing,

(c) section 17 (traffic regulation on special roads), section 25 (pedestrian crossings), Part V (traffic signs) and Part VI (speed limits) of the Road Traffic Regulation Act 1984,
(d) the Road Traffic Act 1988 and the Road Traffic Offenders Act 1988,
(e) the Vehicle Excise and Registration Act 1994,
(f) the Road Traffic (New Drivers) Act 1995, and
(g) the Goods Vehicles (Licensing of Operators) Act 1995.

Regulation of proper hours or periods of work by persons engaged in the carriage of passengers or goods by road.

The conditions under which international road transport services for passengers or goods may be undertaken.

Regulation of the instruction of drivers of motor vehicles.

Exceptions

The subject-matter of sections 39 and 40 (road safety information and training) and 157 to 159 (payments for treatment of traffic casualties) of the Road Traffic Act 1988.

E2. Rail transport

Provision and regulation of railway services.

Rail transport security.

The subject-matter of the Channel Tunnel Act 1987.

The subject-matter of the Railway Heritage Act 1996.

Exceptions

Grants so far as relating to railway services; but this exception does not apply in relation to—

(a) the subject-matter of section 63 of the Railways Act 1993 (government financial assistance where railway administration orders made),
(b) "railway services" as defined in section 82(1)(b) of the Railways Act 1993 (carriage of goods by railway), or
(c) the subject-matter of section 136 of the Railways Act 1993 (grants and subsidies).

Interpretation

"Railway services" has the meaning given by section 82 of the Railways Act 1993 (excluding the wider meaning of "railway" given by section 81(2) of that Act).

E3. Marine transport

The subject-matter of—

(a) the Coastguard Act 1925,
(b) the Hovercraft Act 1968, except so far as relating to the regulation of noise and vibration caused by hovercraft,
(c) the Carriage of Goods by Sea Act 1971,
(d) section 2 of the Protection of Wrecks Act 1973 (prohibition on approaching dangerous wrecks),
(e) the Merchant Shipping (Liner Conferences) Act 1982,
(f) the Dangerous Vessels Act 1985,

(g) the Aviation and Maritime Security Act 1990, other than Part I (aviation security),
(h) the Carriage of Goods by Sea Act 1992,
(i) the Merchant Shipping Act 1995,
(j) the Shipping and Trading Interests (Protection) Act 1995, and
(k) sections 24 (implementation of international agreements relating to protection of wrecks), 26 (piracy) and 27 and 28 (international bodies concerned with maritime matters) of the Merchant Shipping and Maritime Security Act 1997.

Navigational rights and freedoms.

Financial assistance for shipping services which start or finish or both outside Scotland.

Exceptions

Ports, harbours, piers and boatslips, except in relation to the matters reserved by virtue of paragraph (d), (f), (g) or (i).

Regulation of works which may obstruct or endanger navigation.

The subject-matter of the Highlands and Islands Shipping Services Act 1960 in relation to financial assistance for bulk freight services.

E4. Air transport

Regulation of aviation and air transport, including the subject-matter of—

(a) the Carriage by Air Act 1961,
(b) the Carriage by Air (Supplementary Provisions) Act 1962,
(c) the Carriage by Air and Road Act 1979 so far as relating to carriage by air,
(d) the Civil Aviation Act 1982,
(e) the Aviation Security Act 1982,
(f) the Airports Act 1986, and
(g) sections 1 (endangering safety at aerodromes) and 48 (powers in relation to certain aircraft) of the Aviation and Maritime Security Act 1990,

and arrangements to compensate or repatriate passengers in the event of an air transport operator's insolvency.

Exceptions

The subject-matter of the following sections of the Civil Aviation Act 1982—

(a) section 25 (Secretary of State's power to provide aerodromes),
(b) section 30 (provision of aerodromes and facilities at aerodromes by local authorities),
(c) section 31 (power to carry on ancillary business in connection with local authority aerodromes),
(d) section 34 (financial assistance for certain aerodromes),
(e) section 35 (facilities for consultation at certain aerodromes),
(f) section 36 (health control at Secretary of State's aerodromes and aerodromes of Civil Aviation Authority), and
(g) sections 41 to 43 and 50 (powers in relation to land exercisable in connection with civil aviation) where land is to be or was acquired for the purpose of airport development or expansion.

The subject-matter of Part II (transfer of airport undertakings of local authorities), sections 63 and 64 (airport byelaws) and 66 (functions of operators of designated airports as respects abandoned vehicles) of the Airports Act 1986.

The subject-matter of sections 59 (acquisition of land and rights over land) and 60 (disposal of compulsorily acquired land) of the Airports Act 1986 where land is to be or was acquired for the purpose of airport development or expansion.

E5. Other matters

Transport of radioactive material.

Technical specifications for public passenger transport for disabled persons, including the subject-matter of—

(a) section 125(7) and (8) of the Transport Act 1985 (Secretary of State's guidance and consultation with the Disabled Persons Transport Advisory Committee), and

(b) Part V of the Disability Discrimination Act 1995 (public transport).

Regulation of the carriage of dangerous goods.

Interpretation

"Radioactive material" has the same meaning as in section 1(1) of the Radioactive Material (Road Transport) Act 1991.

Head F – Social Security

F1. Social security schemes

Schemes supported from central or local funds which provide assistance for social security purposes to or in respect of individuals by way of benefits.

Requiring persons to—

(a) establish and administer schemes providing assistance for social security purposes to or in respect of individuals, or

(b) make payments to or in respect of such schemes,

and to keep records and supply information in connection with such schemes.

The circumstances in which a person is liable to maintain himself or another for the purposes of the enactments relating to social security and the Child Support Acts 1991 and 1995.

The subject-matter of the Vaccine Damage Payment Scheme.

Illustrations

National Insurance; Social Fund; administration and funding of housing benefit and council tax benefit; recovery of benefits for accident, injury or disease from persons paying damages; deductions from benefits for the purpose of meeting an individual's debts; sharing information between government departments for the purposes of the enactments relating to social security; making decisions for the purposes of schemes mentioned in the reservation and appeals against such decisions.

Exceptions

The subject-matter of Part II of the Social Work (Scotland) Act 1968 (social welfare services), section 2 of the Chronically Sick and Disabled Persons Act 1970 (provision of welfare services), section 50 of the Children Act 1975 (payments towards maintenance of children), section 15 of the Enterprise and New Towns (Scotland) Act 1990 (industrial injuries benefit), and sections 22 (promotion of welfare of children in need), 29 and 30 (advice and assistance for young persons formerly looked after by local authorities) of the Children (Scotland) Act 1995.

Interpretation

"Benefits" includes pensions, allowances, grants, loans and any other form of financial assistance.

Providing assistance for social security purposes to or in respect of individuals includes (among other things) providing assistance to or in respect of individuals—

(a) who qualify by reason of old age, survivorship, disability, sickness, incapacity, injury, unemployment, maternity or the care of children or others needing care,

(b) who qualify by reason of low income, or

(c) in relation to their housing costs or liabilities for local taxes.

F2. Child support

The subject-matter of the Child Support Acts 1991 and 1995.

Exception

The subject-matter of sections 1 to 7 of the Family Law (Scotland) Act 1985 (aliment).

Interpretation

If section 30(2) of the Child Support Act 1991 (collection of payments other than child support maintenance) is not in force on the principal appointed day, it is to be treated for the purposes of this reservation as if it were.

F3. Occupational and personal pensions

The regulation of occupational pension schemes and personal pension schemes, including the obligations of the trustees or managers of such schemes.

Provision about pensions payable to, or in respect of, any persons, except—

(a) the persons referred to in section 81(3),

(b) in relation to a Scottish public authority with mixed functions or no reserved functions, persons who are or have been a member of the public body, the holder of the public office, or a member of the staff of the body, holder or office.

The subject-matter of the Pensions (Increase) Act 1971.

Schemes for the payment of pensions which are listed in Schedule 2 to that Act, except those mentioned in paragraphs 38A and 38AB.

Where pension payable to or in respect of any class of persons under a public service pension scheme is covered by this reservation, so is making provision in their case—

(a) for compensation for loss of office or employment, for their office or employment being affected by constitutional changes, or circumstances arising from such changes, in any territory or territories or for loss or diminution of emoluments, or

(b) for benefits in respect of death or incapacity resulting from injury or disease.

Interpretation

"Pension" includes gratuities and allowances.

F4. War pensions

Schemes for the payment of pensions for or in respect of persons who have a disablement or have died in consequence of service as members of the armed forces of the Crown.

The subject-matter of any scheme under the Personal Injuries (Emergency Provisions) Act 1939, sections 3 to 5 and 7 of the Pensions (Navy, Army, Air Force and Mercantile Marine) Act 1939 or section 1 of the Polish Resettlement Act 1947.

Illustration

The provision of pensions under the Naval, Military and Air Forces Etc. (Disablement and Death) Service Pensions Order 1983.

Interpretation

"Pension" includes grants, allowances, supplements and gratuities.

Head G – Regulation of the Professions

G1. Architects

Regulation of the profession of architect.

G2. Health professions

Regulation of the health professions.

Exceptions

The subject-matter of—

(a) section 21 of the National Health Service (Scotland) Act 1978 (requirement of suitable experience for medical practitioners), and

(b) section 25 of that Act (arrangements for the provision of general dental services), so far as it relates to vocational training and disciplinary proceedings.

Interpretation

"The health professions" means the professions regulated by—

(a) the Pharmacy Act 1954,

(b) the Professions Supplementary to Medicine Act 1960,

(c) the Veterinary Surgeons Act 1966,

(d) the Medical Act 1983,

(e) the Dentists Act 1984,

(f) the Opticians Act 1989,

(g) the Osteopaths Act 1993,

(h) the Chiropractors Act 1994, and

(i) the Nurses, Midwives and Health Visitors Act 1997.

G3. Auditors

Regulation of the profession of auditor.

Head H – Employment

H1. Employment and industrial relations

Employment rights and duties and industrial relations, including the subject-matter of—

(a) the Employers' Liability (Compulsory Insurance) Act 1969,

(b) the Employment Agencies Act 1973,

(c) the Pneumoconiosis etc. (Workers' Compensation) Act 1979,

(d) the Transfer of Undertakings (Protection of Employment) Regulations 1981,
(e) the Trade Union and Labour Relations (Consolidation) Act 1992,
(f) the Industrial Tribunals Act 1996,
(g) the Employment Rights Act 1996, and
(h) the National Minimum Wage Act 1998.

Exception

The subject-matter of the Agricultural Wages (Scotland) Act 1949.

H2. Health and safety

The subject-matter of the following Parts of the Health and Safety at Work etc. Act 1974—

(a) Part I (health, safety and welfare in connection with work, and control of dangerous substances) as extended or applied by section 36 of the Consumer Protection Act 1987, sections 1 and 2 of the Offshore Safety Act 1992 and section 117 of the Railways Act 1993, and
(b) Part II (the Employment Medical Advisory Service).

Exception

Public safety in relation to matters which are not reserved.

H3. Job search and support

The subject-matter of—

(a) the Disabled Persons (Employment) Act 1944, and
(b) the Employment and Training Act 1973, except so far as relating to training for employment.

Exception

The subject-matter of—

(a) sections 8 to 10A of the Employment and Training Act 1973 (careers services), and
(b) the following sections of Part I of the Enterprise and New Towns (Scotland) Act 1990 (Scottish Enterprise and Highlands and Islands Enterprise)—
    (i) section 2(3)(c) (arrangements for the purpose of assisting persons to establish themselves as self-employed persons), and
    (ii) section 12 (disclosure of information).

Head J – Health and Medicines

J1. Abortion

Abortion.

J2. Xenotransplantation

Xenotransplantation.

J3. Embryology, surrogacy and genetics

Surrogacy arrangements, within the meaning of the Surrogacy Arrangements Act 1985, including the subject-matter of that Act.

The subject-matter of the Human Fertilisation and Embryology Act 1990.

Human genetics.

J4. Medicines, medical supplies and poisons

The subject-matter of—

(a) the Medicines Act 1968, the Marketing Authorisations for Veterinary Medicinal Products Regulations 1994 and the Medicines for Human Use (Marketing Authorisations Etc.) Regulations 1994,

(b) the Poisons Act 1972, and

(c) the Biological Standards Act 1975.

Regulation of prices charged for medical supplies or medicinal products which (in either case) are supplied for the purposes of the health service established under section 1 of the National Health Service (Scotland) Act 1978.

Interpretation

"Medical supplies" has the same meaning as in section 49(3) of the National Health Service (Scotland) Act 1978.

"Medicinal products" has the same meaning as in section 130(1) of the Medicines Act 1968.

J5. Welfare foods

Schemes made by regulations under section 13 of the Social Security Act 1988 (schemes for distribution of welfare foods).

Head K – Media and Culture

K1. Broadcasting

The subject-matter of the Broadcasting Act 1990 and the Broadcasting Act 1996.

The British Broadcasting Corporation.

K2. Public lending right

The subject-matter of the Public Lending Right Act 1979.

K3. Government Indemnity Scheme

The subject-matter of sections 16 and 16A of the National Heritage Act 1980 (public indemnities for objects on loan to museums, art galleries, etc.).

K4. Property accepted in satisfaction of tax

The subject-matter of sections 8 and 9 of the National Heritage Act 1980 (payments to Inland Revenue in respect of property accepted in satisfaction of tax, and disposal of such property).

Head L – Miscellaneous

L1. Judicial remuneration

Determination of the remuneration of—

(a) judges of the Court of Session,

(b) sheriffs principal and sheriffs,

(c) members of the Lands Tribunal for Scotland, and

(d) the Chairman of the Scottish Land Court.

L2. Equal opportunities

Equal opportunities, including the subject-matter of—

(a) the Equal Pay Act 1970,

(b) the Sex Discrimination Act 1975,

(c) the Race Relations Act 1976, and
(d) the Disability Discrimination Act 1995.

Exceptions

The encouragement (other than by prohibition or regulation) of equal opportunities, and in particular of the observance of the equal opportunity requirements.

Imposing duties on—

(a) any office-holder in the Scottish Administration, or any Scottish public authority with mixed functions or no reserved functions, to make arrangements with a view to securing that the functions of the office-holder or authority are carried out with due regard to the need to meet the equal opportunity requirements, or
(b) any cross-border public authority to make arrangements with a view to securing that its Scottish functions are carried out with due regard to the need to meet the equal opportunity requirements.

Interpretation

"Equal opportunities" means the prevention, elimination or regulation of discrimination between persons on grounds of sex or marital status, on racial grounds, or on grounds of disability, age, sexual orientation, language or social origin, or of other personal attributes, including beliefs or opinions, such as religious beliefs or political opinions.

"Equal opportunity requirements" means the requirements of the law for the time being relating to equal opportunities.

"Scottish functions" means functions which are exercisable in or as regards Scotland and which do not relate to reserved matters.

L3. Control of weapons

Control of nuclear, biological and chemical weapons and other weapons of mass destruction.

L4. Ordnance survey

The subject-matter of the Ordnance Survey Act 1841.

L5. Time

Timescales, time zones and the subject-matter of the Summer Time Act 1972.

The calendar; units of time; the date of Easter.

Exceptions

The computation of periods of time.

The subject-matter of—

(a) section 1 of the Banking and Financial Dealings Act 1971 (bank holidays), and
(b) the Term and Quarter Days (Scotland) Act 1990.

L6. Outer space

Regulation of activities in outer space.

PART III

GENERAL PROVISIONS

Scottish public authorities

1 (1) This Schedule does not reserve any Scottish public authority if some of its functions relate to reserved matters and some do not, unless it is a cross-border public authority.

(2) Sub-paragraph (1) has effect as regards—

(a) the constitution of the authority, including its establishment and dissolution, its assets and liabilities and its funding and receipts,

(b) conferring or removing any functions specifically exercisable in relation to the authority.

(3) Sub-paragraph (2)(b) does not apply to any function which is specifically exercisable in relation to a particular function of the authority if the particular function relates to reserved matters.

(4) An authority to which this paragraph applies is referred to in this Act as a Scottish public authority with mixed functions.

2 Paragraph 1 of Part I of this Schedule does not reserve any Scottish public authority with functions none of which relate to reserved matters (referred to in this Act as a Scottish public authority with no reserved functions).

Reserved bodies

3 (1) The reservation of any body to which this paragraph applies has effect to reserve—

(a) its constitution, including its establishment and dissolution, its assets and liabilities and its funding and receipts,

(b) conferring functions on it or removing functions from it,

(c) conferring or removing any functions specifically exercisable in relation to it.

(2) This paragraph applies to—

(a) a body reserved by name by Part II of this Schedule,

(b) each of the councils reserved by Section C12 of that Part,

(c) the Commission for Racial Equality, the Equal Opportunities Commission and the National Disability Council.

Financial assistance to industry

4 (1) This Schedule does not reserve giving financial assistance to commercial activities for the purpose of promoting or sustaining economic development or employment.

(2) Sub-paragraph (1)—

(a) does not apply to giving financial assistance to any activities in pursuance of a power exercisable only in relation to activities which are reserved,

(b) does not apply to Part I of this Schedule, except paragraph 9, or to a body to which paragraph 3 of this Part of this Schedule applies,

(c) is without prejudice to the exceptions from the reservations in Sections E2 and E3 of Part II of this Schedule.

(3) Sub-paragraph (1) does not affect the question whether any matter other than financial assistance to which that sub-paragraph applies is reserved.

Interpretation

5 (1) References in this Schedule to the subject-matter of any enactment are to be read as references to the subject-matter of that enactment as it has effect on the principal appointed day or, if it ceased to have effect at any time within the period ending with that day and beginning with the day on which this Act is passed, as it had effect immediately before that time.

(2) Subordinate legislation under section 129(1) may, in relation to the operation of this Schedule at any time before the principal appointed day, modify the references to that day in sub-paragraph (1).

SCHEDULE 6

Section 98.

DEVOLUTION ISSUES

PART I

PRELIMINARY

1 In this Schedule "devolution issue" means—

(a) a question whether an Act of the Scottish Parliament or any provision of an Act of the Scottish Parliament is within the legislative competence of the Parliament,

(b) a question whether any function (being a function which any person has purported, or is proposing, to exercise) is a function of the Scottish Ministers, the First Minister or the Lord Advocate,

(c) a question whether the purported or proposed exercise of a function by a member of the Scottish Executive is, or would be, within devolved competence,

(d) a question whether a purported or proposed exercise of a function by a member of the Scottish Executive is, or would be, incompatible with any of the Convention rights or with Community law,

(e) a question whether a failure to act by a member of the Scottish Executive is incompatible with any of the Convention rights or with Community law,

(f) any other question about whether a function is exercisable within devolved competence or in or as regards Scotland and any other question arising by virtue of this Act about reserved matters.

2 A devolution issue shall not be taken to arise in any proceedings merely because of any contention of a party to the proceedings which appears to the court or tribunal before which the proceedings take place to be frivolous or vexatious.

PART II

PROCEEDINGS IN SCOTLAND

Application of Part II

3 This Part of this Schedule applies in relation to devolution issues in proceedings in Scotland.

Institution of proceedings

4 (1) Proceedings for the determination of a devolution issue may be instituted by the Advocate General or the Lord Advocate.

(2) The Lord Advocate may defend any such proceedings instituted by the Advocate General.

(3) This paragraph is without prejudice to any power to institute or defend proceedings exercisable apart from this paragraph by any person.

Intimation of devolution issue

5 Intimation of any devolution issue which arises in any proceedings before a court or tribunal shall be given to the Advocate General and the Lord Advocate (unless the person to whom the intimation would be given is a party to the proceedings).

6 A person to whom intimation is given in pursuance of paragraph 5 may take part as a party in the proceedings, so far as they relate to a devolution issue.

Reference of devolution issue to higher court

7 A court, other than the House of Lords or any court consisting of three or more judges of the Court of Session, may refer any devolution issue which arises in proceedings (other than criminal proceedings) before it to the Inner House of the Court of Session.

8 A tribunal from which there is no appeal shall refer any devolution issue which arises in proceedings before it to the Inner House of the Court of Session; and any other tribunal may make such a reference.

9 A court, other than any court consisting of two or more judges of the High Court of Justiciary, may refer any devolution issue which arises in criminal proceedings before it to the High Court of Justiciary.

References from superior courts to Judicial Committee

10 Any court consisting of three or more judges of the Court of Session may refer any devolution issue which arises in proceedings before it (otherwise than on a reference under paragraph 7 or 8) to the Judicial Committee.

11 Any court consisting of two or more judges of the High Court of Justiciary may refer any devolution issue which arises in proceedings before it (otherwise than on a reference under paragraph 9) to the Judicial Committee.

Appeals from superior courts to Judicial Committee

12 An appeal against a determination of a devolution issue by the Inner House of the Court of Session on a reference under paragraph 7 or 8 shall lie to the Judicial Committee.

13 An appeal against a determination of a devolution issue by—

(a) a court of two or more judges of the High Court of Justiciary (whether in the ordinary course of proceedings or on a reference under paragraph 9), or

(b) a court of three or more judges of the Court of Session from which there is no appeal to the House of Lords,

shall lie to the Judicial Committee, but only with leave of the court concerned or, failing such leave, with special leave of the Judicial Committee.

PART III

PROCEEDINGS IN ENGLAND AND WALES

Application of Part III

14 This Part of this Schedule applies in relation to devolution issues in proceedings in England and Wales.

Institution of proceedings

15 (1) Proceedings for the determination of a devolution issue may be instituted by the Attorney General.

(2) The Lord Advocate may defend any such proceedings.

(3) This paragraph is without prejudice to any power to institute or defend proceedings exercisable apart from this paragraph by any person.

Notice of devolution issue

16 A court or tribunal shall order notice of any devolution issue which arises in any proceedings before it to be given to the Attorney General and the Lord Advocate (unless the person to whom the notice would be given is a party to the proceedings).

17 A person to whom notice is given in pursuance of paragraph 16 may take part as a party in the proceedings, so far as they relate to a devolution issue.

Reference of devolution issue to High Court or Court of Appeal

18 A magistrates' court may refer any devolution issue which arises in proceedings (other than criminal proceedings) before it to the High Court.

19 (1) A court may refer any devolution issue which arises in proceedings (other than criminal proceedings) before it to the Court of Appeal.

(2) Sub-paragraph (1) does not apply to—

(a) a magistrates' court, the Court of Appeal or the House of Lords, or

(b) the High Court if the devolution issue arises in proceedings on a reference under paragraph 18.

20 A tribunal from which there is no appeal shall refer any devolution issue which arises in proceedings before it to the Court of Appeal; and any other tribunal may make such a reference.

21 A court, other than the House of Lords or the Court of Appeal, may refer any devolution issue which arises in criminal proceedings before it to—

(a) the High Court (if the proceedings are summary proceedings), or

(b) the Court of Appeal (if the proceedings are proceedings on indictment).

References from Court of Appeal to Judicial Committee

22 The Court of Appeal may refer any devolution issue which arises in proceedings before it (otherwise than on a reference under paragraph 19, 20 or 21) to the Judicial Committee.

Appeals from superior courts to Judicial Committee

23 An appeal against a determination of a devolution issue by the High Court or the Court of Appeal on a reference under paragraph 18, 19, 20 or 21 shall lie to the Judicial Committee, but only with leave of the High Court or (as the case may be) the Court of Appeal or, failing such leave, with special leave of the Judicial Committee.

Part IV

Proceedings in Northern Ireland

Application of Part IV

24 This Part of this Schedule applies in relation to devolution issues in proceedings in Northern Ireland.

Institution of proceedings

25 (1) Proceedings for the determination of a devolution issue may be instituted by the Attorney General for Northern Ireland.

(2) The Lord Advocate may defend any such proceedings.

(3) This paragraph is without prejudice to any power to institute or defend proceedings exercisable apart from this paragraph by any person.

Notice of devolution issue

26 A court or tribunal shall order notice of any devolution issue which arises in any proceedings before it to be given to the Attorney General for Northern Ireland and the Lord Advocate (unless the person to whom the notice would be given is a party to the proceedings).

27 A person to whom notice is given in pursuance of paragraph 26 may take part as a party in the proceedings, so far as they relate to a devolution issue.

Reference of devolution issue to Court of Appeal

28 A court, other than the House of Lords or the Court of Appeal in Northern Ireland, may refer any devolution issue which arises in any proceedings before it to the Court of Appeal in Northern Ireland.

29 A tribunal from which there is no appeal shall refer any devolution issue which arises in any proceedings before it to the Court of Appeal in Northern Ireland; and any other tribunal may make such a reference.

References from Court of Appeal to Judicial Committee

30 The Court of Appeal in Northern Ireland may refer any devolution issue which arises in proceedings before it (otherwise than on a reference under paragraph 28 or 29) to the Judicial Committee.

Appeals from Court of Appeal to Judicial Committee

31 An appeal against a determination of a devolution issue by the Court of Appeal in Northern Ireland on a reference under paragraph 28 or 29 shall lie to the Judicial Committee, but only with leave of the Court of Appeal in Northern Ireland or, failing such leave, with special leave of the Judicial Committee.

PART V

GENERAL

Proceedings in the House of Lords

32 Any devolution issue which arises in judicial proceedings in the House of Lords shall be referred to the Judicial Committee unless the House considers it more appropriate, having regard to all the circumstances, that it should determine the issue.

Direct references to Judicial Committee

33 The Lord Advocate, the Advocate General, the Attorney General or the Attorney General for Northern Ireland may require any court or tribunal to refer to the Judicial Committee any devolution issue which has arisen in proceedings before it to which he is a party.

34 The Lord Advocate, the Attorney General, the Advocate General or the Attorney General for Northern Ireland may refer to the Judicial Committee any devolution issue which is not the subject of proceedings.

35 (1) This paragraph applies where a reference is made under paragraph 34 in relation to a devolution issue which relates to the proposed exercise of a function by a member of the Scottish Executive.

(2) The person making the reference shall notify a member of the Scottish Executive of that fact.

(3) No member of the Scottish Executive shall exercise the function in the manner proposed during the period beginning with the receipt of the notification under sub-paragraph (2) and ending with the reference being decided or otherwise disposed of.

(4) Proceedings relating to any possible failure by a member of the Scottish Executive to comply with sub-paragraph (3) may be instituted by the Advocate General.

(5) Sub-paragraph (4) is without prejudice to any power to institute proceedings exercisable apart from that sub-paragraph by any person.

Expenses

36 (1) A court or tribunal before which any proceedings take place may take account of any additional expense of the kind mentioned in sub-paragraph (3) in deciding any question as to costs or expenses.

(2) In deciding any such question, the court or tribunal may award the whole or part of the additional expense as costs or (as the case may be) expenses to the party who incurred it (whatever the decision on the devolution issue).

(3) The additional expense is any additional expense which the court or tribunal considers that any party to the proceedings has incurred as a result of the participation of any person in pursuance of paragraph 6, 17 or 27.

Procedure of courts and tribunals

37 Any power to make provision for regulating the procedure before any court or tribunal shall include power to make provision for the purposes of this Schedule including, in particular, provision—

(a) for prescribing the stage in the proceedings at which a devolution issue is to be raised or referred,

(b) for the sisting or staying of proceedings for the purpose of any proceedings under this Schedule, and

(c) for determining the manner in which and the time within which any intimation or notice is to be given.

Interpretation

38 Any duty or power conferred by this Schedule to refer a devolution issue to a court shall be construed as a duty or (as the case may be) power to refer the issue to the court for decision.

SCHEDULE 7

Section 115.

PROCEDURE FOR SUBORDINATE LEGISLATION

General provision

1 (1) Subordinate legislation (or a statutory instrument containing it) under a provision listed in the left-hand column is subject to the type of procedure in the right-hand column.

(2) This paragraph is subject to paragraphs 3 and 4.

Provision of the Act	*Type of procedure*
Section 2(1)	Type C
Section 12(1)	Type C
Section 15	Type D
Section 18(5)	Type J
Section 30	Type A
Section 35	Type I
Section 38	Type J
Section 56(2)	Type G
Section 58	Type I
Section 60	Type G
Section 62	Type G
Section 63	Type A
Section 64(5)	Type K
Section 67(3)	Type E
Section 71(6)	Type K
Section 79	Type E
Section 88	Type I
Section 89	Type F
Section 90	Type F
Section 93	Type H
Section 97	Type A
Section 103(3)(a) and (b)	Type I
Section 104	Type G
Section 105	Type G
Section 106	Type G
Section 107	Type G
Section 108	Type A
Section 109	Type H
Section 110(1)	Type C

Notes

The entry for section 58 does not apply to an instrument containing an order merely revoking an order under subsection (1) of that section.

The entry for section 79, in relation to an instrument containing an order which makes only such provision as is mentioned in section 79(3), is to be read as referring to type K instead of type E.

Provision of the Act	*Type of procedure*
Section 110(2)	Type I
Section 111	Type A
Section 116(9)	Type G
Section 124(1)	Type G
Section 126(2)	Type B
Section 126(8)	Type H
Section 129(1)	Type G
Schedule 2, paragraph 2	Type G
Schedule 2, paragraph 7	Type H

Notes

The entry for section 58 does not apply to an instrument containing an order merely revoking an order under subsection (1) of that section.

The entry for section 79, in relation to an instrument containing an order which makes only such provision as is mentioned in section 79(3), is to be read as referring to type K instead of type E.

Types of procedure

2 The types of procedure referred to in this Schedule are—

Type A: No recommendation to make the legislation is to be made to Her Majesty in Council unless a draft of the instrument —

(a) has been laid before, and approved by resolution of, each House of Parliament, and

(b) has been laid before, and approved by resolution of, the Parliament.

Type B: No recommendation to make the legislation is to be made to Her Majesty in Council unless a draft of the instrument has been laid before, and approved by resolution of, each House of Parliament.

Type C: No Minister of the Crown is to make the legislation unless a draft of the instrument has been laid before, and approved by resolution of, each House of Parliament.

Type D: No recommendation to make the legislation is to be made to Her Majesty in Council unless a draft of the instrument has been laid before, and approved by resolution of, the Parliament.

Type E: No Minister of the Crown is to make the legislation unless a draft of the instrument has been laid before, and approved by resolution of, the House of Commons.

Type F: The instrument containing the legislation, if made without a draft having been approved by resolution of each House of Parliament and of the Parliament, shall be subject to annulment in pursuance of—

(a) a resolution of either House, or

(b) a resolution of the Parliament.

Type G: The instrument containing the legislation, if made without a draft having been approved by resolution of each House of Parliament, shall be subject to annulment in pursuance of a resolution of either House.

Type H: The instrument containing the legislation shall be subject to annulment in pursuance of—

(a) a resolution of either House of Parliament, or

(b) a resolution of the Parliament.

Type I: The instrument containing the legislation shall be subject to annulment in pursuance of a resolution of either House of Parliament.

Type J: The instrument containing the legislation shall be subject to annulment in pursuance of a resolution of the Parliament.

Type K: The instrument containing the legislation shall be subject to annulment in pursuance of a resolution of the House of Commons.

Special cases

3 (1) This paragraph applies if—

(a) the instrument containing the legislation would, apart from this paragraph, be subject to the type F, G, H, I or K procedure, and

(b) the legislation contains provisions which add to, replace or omit any part of the text of an Act.

(2) Where this paragraph applies—

(a) instead of the type F procedure, the type A procedure shall apply,

(b) instead of the type G procedure, the type B or (as the case may be) C procedure shall apply,

(c) instead of the type H procedure, the type A procedure shall apply,

(d) instead of the type I procedure, the type B or (as the case may be) C procedure shall apply,

(e) instead of the type K procedure, the type E procedure shall apply.

4 If legislation under section 129(1) makes provision as mentioned in section 112(2) then, instead of the type G procedure, the type D procedure shall apply.

5 (1) An instrument containing an Order in Council or order under an open power which revokes, amends or re-enacts subordinate legislation under an open power may (in spite of section 14 of the Interpretation Act 1978) be subject to a different procedure under this Schedule from the procedure to which the instrument containing the original legislation was subject.

(2) An instrument containing an Order in Council under section 89 or 90 which revokes, amends or re-enacts an Order under either section may (in spite of section 14 of the Interpretation Act 1978) be subject to a different procedure under this Schedule from the procedure to which the instrument containing the original Order was subject.

SCHEDULE 8

Section 125.

MODIFICATIONS OF ENACTMENTS

Public Revenue (Scotland) Act 1833 (c. 13)

1 In section 2 of the Public Revenue (Scotland) Act 1833 (regulation of Queen's and Lord Treasurer's Remembrancer), for "Treasury" in both places there is substituted "Scottish Ministers".

Crown Suits (Scotland) Act 1857 (c. 44)

2 (1) The Crown Suits (Scotland) Act 1857 is amended as follows.

(2) In section 1 (Crown suits may be brought by or against Lord Advocate)—

(a) after "Crown" there is inserted "(including the Scottish Administration)", and

(b) for "Her Majesty's Advocate for the time being" there is substituted "the appropriate Law Officer".

(3) In section 2 (authority of Crown required)—

(a) for "Her Majesty's Advocate" there is substituted "the appropriate Law Officer", and

(b) after "Majesty" there is inserted "of the part of the Scottish Administration".

(4) In section 3 (absence of authority cannot be founded upon), for "Her Majesty's Advocate" there is substituted "the appropriate Law Officer".

(5) After section 4 there is inserted—

"4A Meaning of "the appropriate Law Officer"

"4A "4A Meaning of "the appropriate Law Officer"

In this Act "the appropriate Law Officer" means—

(a) the Lord Advocate, where the action, suit or proceeding is on behalf of or against any part of the Scottish Administration, and

(b) the Advocate General for Scotland, in any other case."

(6) In section 5 (change of Lord Advocate not to affect proceedings)—

(a) for "Her Majesty's Advocate" there is substituted "the Lord Advocate or the Advocate General for Scotland", and

(b) for "the office of Her Majesty's Advocate" there is substituted "that office".

Sheriff Courts and Legal Officers (Scotland) Act 1927 (c. 35)

3 (1) The Sheriff Courts and Legal Officers (Scotland) Act 1927 is amended as follows.

(2) In section 1(2) (appointment etc. of procurator fiscal), "with the consent of the Treasury" is omitted.

(3) In section 2 (appointment of sheriff clerk and procurator fiscal deputes), "with the consent of the Treasury as to numbers and salaries" is omitted.

(4) In section 3 (whole-time sheriff clerks and procurators fiscal and deputes), "and in either case with the consent of the Treasury" is omitted.

(5) In section 5 (whole-time clerks), "with the consent of the Treasury as to numbers and salaries" is omitted.

(6) In section 12 (prosecutions at instance of procurator fiscal), "after consultation with the Treasury" is omitted.

Administration of Justice (Scotland) Act 1933 (c. 41)

4 In the Administration of Justice (Scotland) Act 1933, in sections 24(7) and 25 (officers of Court of Session etc.), "and shall be exercised on nomination by the Lord Advocate" is omitted.

Private Legislation Procedure (Scotland) Act 1936 (c. 52)

5 In section 1 of the Private Legislation Procedure (Scotland) Act 1936 (application for provisional order: notices), after subsection (4) there is added—

"(5) This section shall not apply where any public authority or any persons desire to obtain parliamentary powers the conferring of which is wholly within the legislative competence of the Scottish Parliament."

United Nations Act 1946 (c. 45)

6 In section 1 of the United Nations Act 1946 (measures to give effect to decisions of Security Council), in subsection (4), for the words following "shall" there is substituted "forthwith after it is made be laid—

(a) before Parliament; and

(b) if any provision made by the Order would, if it were included in an Act of the Scottish Parliament, be within the legislative competence of that Parliament, before that Parliament."

Crown Proceedings Act 1947 (c. 44)

7 (1) The Crown Proceedings Act 1947 is amended as follows.

(2) In section 38(2) (interpretation)—

(a) in the definition of "His Majesty's aircraft", after "Kingdom" there is inserted "or the Scottish Administration",

(b) in the definition of "His Majesty's ships", after "Kingdom" there is inserted "or the Scottish Administration" and after "said Government" there is inserted "or Administration", and

(c) in the definition of "officer", after "Minister of the Crown" there is inserted "and a member of the Scottish Executive".

(3) In section 40 (savings)—

(a) in subsection (2), after "in the United Kingdom", in each place where those words appear, there is inserted "or the Scottish Administration", and

(b) after subsection (3) there is inserted—

"(3A) A certificate of the Scottish Ministers to the effect that—

(a) any alleged liability of the Crown arises otherwise than in respect of the Scottish Administration,

(b) any proceedings by the Crown are proceedings otherwise than in right of the Scottish Administration,

shall, for the purposes of this Act, be conclusive as to that matter."

(4) In the proviso to section 44 (remit from sheriff court to Court of Session on Lord Advocate's certificate)—

(a) for "Lord Advocate" there is substituted "appropriate Law Officer", and

(b) at the end there is inserted—

"In this proviso, "the appropriate Law Officer" means—

(a) the Lord Advocate, where the proceedings are against any part of the Scottish Administration, and

(b) the Advocate General for Scotland, in any other case."

(5) In section 50 (application to Scotland of section 35), subsection (2) of section 35 as substituted for Scotland is amended as follows—

(a) in paragraph (d)—

(i) after "Crown" there is inserted "in right of Her Majesty's Government in the United Kingdom",

(ii) for "Lord Advocate" there is substituted "Advocate General for Scotland", and

(iii) after "department", in the second place where it appears, there is inserted—

"(i) shall not be entitled to avail itself of any set-off or counterclaim if the subject matter thereof relates to the Scottish Administration, and

(ii)",

and

(b) after that paragraph there is inserted—

"(e) a part of the Scottish Administration, in any proceedings against that part or against the Lord Advocate on its behalf, shall not be entitled to avail itself of any set-off or counterclaim if the subject matter thereof relates to another part of the Scottish Administration or to the Crown in right of Her Majesty's Government in the United Kingdom."

(6) In section 51(2) (application to Scotland of section 38), in paragraph (ii), after "Lord Advocate" there is inserted "or the Advocate General for Scotland".

Public Registers and Records (Scotland) Act 1948 (c. 57)

8 In section 1(1) of the Public Registers and Records (Scotland) Act 1948 (appointment etc. of Keeper of the Registers and Keeper of the Records), for "Secretary of State" there is substituted "Scottish Ministers".

Lands Tribunal Act 1949 (c. 42)

9 In section 2 of the Lands Tribunal Act 1949 (members etc. of Lands Tribunal for Scotland)—

(a) in subsection (9)—

(i) after "effect" there is inserted "with the omission of subsection (8) and", and

(ii) in paragraph (a), for "(8)" there is substituted "(7)", and

(b) after that subsection there is inserted—

"(10) The remuneration of members of the Lands Tribunal for Scotland shall be charged on the Scottish Consolidated Fund."

Defamation Act 1952 (c. 66)

10 In section 10 of the Defamation Act 1952 (limitation on privilege at elections), after "local government authority" there is inserted "to the Scottish Parliament".

Defamation Act (Northern Ireland) 1955 (c. 11 (N.I.))

11 In section 10(2) of the Defamation Act (Northern Ireland) 1955 (limitation on privilege at elections), after "Parliament of the United Kingdom" there is inserted "or to the Scottish Parliament".

Registration of Births, Deaths and Marriages (Scotland) Act 1965 (c. 49)

12 In section 1(1) of the Registration of Births, Deaths and Marriages (Scotland) Act 1965 (power of Secretary of State to appoint Registrar General), for "Secretary of State" there is substituted "Scottish Ministers".

Pensions (Increase) Act 1971 (c. 56)

13 In Part II of Schedule 2 to the Pensions (Increase) Act 1971 (official pensions out of local funds), before paragraph 39 there is inserted—

"Scottish Parliament and Scottish Executive

38AB A pension payable under a scheme established by virtue of section 81(4)(b) of, or paragraph 3(4)(b) of Schedule 2 to, the Scotland Act 1998."

Superannuation Act 1972 (c. 11)

14 In section 1(6) of the Superannuation Act 1972 (superannuation as respects civil servants etc.), for "or the Consolidated Fund" there is substituted "the Consolidated Fund or the Scottish Consolidated Fund".

European Communities Act 1972 (c. 68)

15 (1) The European Communities Act 1972 is amended as follows.

(2) In section 2 (general implementation of Treaties)—

(a) references to a statutory power or duty include a power or duty conferred by an Act of the Scottish Parliament or an instrument made under such an Act, and

(b) references to an enactment include an enactment within the meaning of this Act.

(3) In relation to regulations made by the Scottish Ministers, or an Order in Council made on the recommendation of the First Minister, under section 2—

(a) in subsection (2), "designated" in the first sentence, and the second sentence, shall be disregarded,

(b) references to an Act of Parliament shall be read as references to an Act of the Scottish Parliament, and

(c) paragraph 2(2) of Schedule 2 shall have effect as if the references to each, or either, House of Parliament were to the Scottish Parliament.

(4) In section 3(4) (evidence), references to a government department include any part of the Scottish Administration.

Interpretation Act 1978 (c. 30)

16 (1) The Interpretation Act 1978 is amended as follows.

(2) After section 23 there is inserted—

"23A Acts of the Scottish Parliament etc

"23A "23A Acts of the Scottish Parliament etc

(1) This Act applies in relation to an Act of the Scottish Parliament and an instrument made under such an Act only to the extent provided in this section.

(2) Except as provided in subsection (3) below, sections 15 to 18 apply to—

(a) an Act of the Scottish Parliament as they apply to an Act,

(b) an instrument made under an Act of the Scottish Parliament as they apply to subordinate legislation.

(3) In the application of those sections to an Act and to subordinate legislation—

(a) references to an enactment include an enactment comprised in, or in an instrument made under, an Act of the Scottish Parliament, and

(b) the reference in section 17(2)(b) to subordinate legislation includes an instrument made under an Act of the Scottish Parliament.

(4) In the application of section 20 to an Act and to subordinate legislation, references to an enactment include an enactment comprised in, or in an instrument made under, an Act of the Scottish Parliament."

(3) In Schedule 1 (words and expressions defined), the following definitions are inserted in the appropriate places—

"""Act" means an Act of Parliament."

"""Enactment" does not include an enactment comprised in, or in an instrument made under, an Act of the Scottish Parliament."

Education (Scotland) Act 1980 (c. 44)

17 In section 135(1) of the Education (Scotland) Act 1980 (interpretation), in the definition of "Her Majesty's inspectors", "on the recommendation of the Secretary of State" is omitted.

Civil Jurisdiction and Judgments Act 1982 (c. 27)

18 (1) Section 46 of the Civil Jurisdiction and Judgments Act 1982 (domicile and seat of the Crown) is amended as follows.

(2) In subsection (3), after paragraph (a) there is inserted—

"(aa) the Crown in right of the Scottish Administration has its seat in, and in every place in, Scotland,".

(3) In subsection (7), after "Kingdom" there is inserted ", the Scottish Administration".

Mental Health Act 1983 (c. 20)

19 In section 141 of the Mental Health Act 1983 (members of the House of Commons suffering from mental illness), after subsection (7), there is added—

"(8) This section also has effect in relation to members of the Scottish Parliament but as if—

(a) any references to the House of Commons or the Speaker were references to the Scottish Parliament or (as the case may be) the Presiding Officer, and

(b) subsection (7) were omitted."

National Audit Act 1983 (c. 44)

20 Sections 6 and 7 of the National Audit Act 1983 (value for money studies) shall not apply in relation to—

(a) the Scottish Administration or any part of it, or

(b) any Scottish public authority with mixed functions or no reserved functions.

Tourism (Overseas Promotion) (Scotland) Act 1984 (c. 4)

21 In section 1 of the Tourism (Overseas Promotion) (Scotland) Act 1984 (power of Scottish Tourist Board to promote tourism in Scotland outside UK), subsection (2) is omitted.

Bankruptcy (Scotland) Act 1985 (c. 66)

22 For section 1 of the Bankruptcy (Scotland) Act 1985 there is substituted—

"1 Accountant in Bankruptcy

"1 "1 Accountant in Bankruptcy

(1) The Accountant in Bankruptcy shall be appointed by the Scottish Ministers.

(2) The Scottish Ministers may appoint a member of the staff of the Accountant in Bankruptcy to be Depute Accountant in Bankruptcy to exercise all of the functions of the Accountant in Bankruptcy at any time when the Accountant in Bankruptcy is unable to do so."

Insolvency Act 1986 (c. 45)

23 (1) The Insolvency Act 1986 is amended as follows.

(2) Anything directed to be done, or which may be done, to or by—

(a) the registrar of companies in Scotland by virtue of any of the provisions mentioned in sub-paragraph (3), or

(b) the assistant registrar of friendly societies for Scotland by virtue of any of those provisions as applied (with or without modification) in relation to friendly societies, industrial and provident societies or building societies,

shall, or (as the case may be) may, also be done to or by the Accountant in Bankruptcy.

(3) Those provisions are: sections 53(1), 54(3), 61(6), 62(5) (so far as relating to the giving of notice), 67(1), 69(2), 84(3), 94(3), 106(3) and (5), 112(3), 130(1), 147(3), 170(2) and 172(8).

(4) Anything directed to be done to or by—

(a) the registrar of companies in Scotland by virtue of any of the provisions mentioned in sub-paragraph (5), or

(b) the assistant registrar of friendly societies for Scotland by virtue of any of those provisions as applied (with or without modification) in relation to friendly societies, industrial and provident societies or building societies,

shall instead be done to or by the Accountant in Bankruptcy.

(5) Those provisions are: sections 89(3), 109(1), 171(5) and (6), 173(2)(a) and 192(1).

(6) In section 427 (members of the House of Commons whose estates are sequestrated etc.), after subsection (6) there is inserted—

"(6A) Subsections (4) to (6) have effect in relation to a member of the Scottish Parliament but as if—

(a) references to the House of Commons were to the Parliament and references to the Speaker were to the Presiding Officer, and

(b) in subsection (4), for "under this section" there were substituted "under section 15(1)(b) of the Scotland Act 1998 by virtue of this section"."

Public Order Act 1986 (c. 64)

24 In section 26(1) of the Public Order Act 1986 (savings for reports of parliamentary proceedings), after "Parliament" there is inserted "or in the Scottish Parliament".

Copyright, Designs and Patents Act 1988 (c. 48)

25 (1) The Copyright, Designs and Patents Act 1988 is amended as follows.

(2) In section 12(9) (duration of copyright in literary, dramatic, musical or artistic works), for "166" there is substituted "166A".

(3) In section 153(2) (qualification for copyright protection), for "166" there is substituted "166A".

(4) In section 163(6) (Crown copyright), for "and 166" there is substituted "to 166A".

(5) In section 164(1) (Crown copyright in Acts of Parliament etc.), after "Parliament" there is inserted "Act of the Scottish Parliament".

(6) After section 166 there is inserted—

"166A Copyright in Bills of the Scottish Parliament

"166A "166A Copyright in Bills of the Scottish Parliament

(1) Copyright in every Bill introduced into the Scottish Parliament belongs to the Scottish Parliamentary Corporate Body.

(2) Copyright under this section subsists from the time when the text of the Bill is handed in to the Parliament for introduction—

(a) until the Bill receives Royal Assent, or

(b) if the Bill does not receive Royal Assent, until it is withdrawn or rejected or no further parliamentary proceedings may be taken in respect of it.

(3) References in this Part to Parliamentary copyright (except in section 165) include copyright under this section; and, except as mentioned above, the provisions of this Part apply in relation to copyright under this section as to other Parliamentary copyright.

(4) No other copyright, or right in the nature of copyright, subsists in a Bill after copyright has once subsisted under this section; but without prejudice to the subsequent operation of this section in relation to a Bill which, not having received Royal Assent, is later reintroduced into the Parliament."

(7) In section 178 (minor definitions)—

(a) in the definition of "the Crown", after "of" there is inserted "the Scottish Administration or of", and

(b) in the definition of "parliamentary proceedings", after "Assembly" there is inserted "of the Scottish Parliament".

(8) In section 179 (index of defined expressions), in column 2 of the entry for "Parliamentary copyright", for "and 166(6)" there is substituted "166(6) and 166A(3)".

Official Secrets Act 1989 (c. 6)

26 (1) Section 12 of the Official Secrets Act 1989 (meaning of "Crown servant" and "government contractor" for the purposes of that Act) is amended as follows.

(2) In subsection (1), after paragraph (a) there is inserted—

"(aa) a member of the Scottish Executive or a junior Scottish Minister;".

(3) In subsection (2)(a), after "above," there is inserted "of any office-holder in the Scottish Administration,".

(4) After subsection (3) there is inserted—

"(4) In this section "office-holder in the Scottish Administration" has the same meaning as in section 126(7)(a) of the Scotland Act 1998.".

Prisons (Scotland) Act 1989 (c. 45)

27 (1) The Prisons (Scotland) Act 1989 is amended as follows.

(2) Section 2 of that Act (appointment of officers etc.) is omitted.

(3) In section 3(1) (prison officers), for the words following "Secretary of State" there is substituted—

"(1A) Every prison shall have a governor and such other officers as may be necessary."

(4) In section 3A (medical services)—

(a) in subsection (2), for "appointing" there is substituted "providing" and for "appointment" there is substituted "provision", and

(b) in subsection (4), for "appointed" there is substituted "provided".

European Communities (Amendment) Act 1993 (c. 32)

28 In section 6 of the European Communities (Amendment) Act 1993 (persons who may be proposed for membership of the Committee of the Regions), after "he is" there is inserted "a member of the Scottish Parliament".

Scottish Land Court Act 1993 (c. 45)

29 In section 1 of the Scottish Land Court Act 1993 (the Scottish Land Court)—

(a) in subsection (2), for "Secretary of State" there is substituted "First Minister", and

(b) after subsection (2) there is inserted—

"(2A) Before recommending the appointment of a person as Chairman, the First Minister shall consult the Lord President of the Court of Session."

Value Added Tax Act 1994 (c. 23)

30 In section 41 of the Value Added Tax Act 1994 (application to the Crown), in subsection (6), after "includes" there is inserted "the Scottish Administration".

Requirements of Writing (Scotland) Act 1995 (c. 7)

31 In section 12(1) of the Requirements of Writing (Scotland) Act 1995 (interpretation) —

(a) in the definition of "Minister", after "1975" there is inserted "and also includes a member of the Scottish Executive", and

(b) in paragraph (a) of the definition of "officer", after "Department" there is inserted "or, as the case may be, as a member of the staff of the Scottish Ministers or the Lord Advocate".

Criminal Procedure (Scotland) Act 1995 (c. 46)

32 (1) The Criminal Procedure (Scotland) Act 1995 is amended as follows.

(2) After section 288 there is inserted—

"Devolution issues

288A Rights of appeal for Advocate General: devolution issues

288A 288A Rights of appeal for Advocate General: devolution issues

(1) This section applies where—

(a) a person is acquitted or convicted of a charge (whether on indictment or in summary proceedings), and

(b) the Advocate General for Scotland was a party to the proceedings in pursuance of paragraph 6 of Schedule 6 to the Scotland Act 1998 (devolution issues).

(2) The Advocate General for Scotland may refer any devolution issue which has arisen in the proceedings to the High Court for their opinion; and the Clerk of Justiciary shall send to the person acquitted or convicted and to any solicitor who acted for that person at the trial, a copy of the reference and intimation of the date fixed by the Court for a hearing.

(3) The person may, not later than seven days before the date so fixed, intimate in writing to the Clerk of Justiciary and to the Advocate General for Scotland either—

(a) that he elects to appear personally at the hearing, or

(b) that he elects to be represented by counsel at the hearing,

but, except by leave of the Court on cause shown, and without prejudice to his right to attend, he shall not appear or be represented at the hearing other than by and in conformity with an election under this subsection.

(4) Where there is no intimation under subsection (3)(b), the High Court shall appoint counsel to act at the hearing as amicus curiae.

(5) The costs of representation elected under subsection (3)(b) or of an appointment under subsection (4) shall, after being taxed by the Auditor of the Court of Session, be paid by the Advocate General for Scotland out of money provided by Parliament.

(6) The opinion on the point referred under subsection (2) shall not affect the acquittal or (as the case may be) conviction in the trial.

288B Appeals to Judicial Committee of the Privy Council

288B 288B Appeals to Judicial Committee of the Privy Council

(1) This section applies where the Judicial Committee of the Privy Council determines an appeal under paragraph 13(a) of Schedule 6 to the Scotland Act 1998 against a determination of a devolution issue by the High Court in the ordinary course of proceedings.

(2) The determination of the appeal shall not affect any earlier acquittal or earlier quashing of any conviction in the proceedings.

(3) Subject to subsection (2) above, the High Court shall have the same powers in relation to the proceedings when remitted to it by the Judicial Committee as it would have if it were considering the proceedings otherwise than as a trial court."

(3) In section 307(1) (interpretation), after the definition of "crime" there is inserted—

""devolution issue" has the same meaning as in Schedule 6 to the Scotland Act 1998;".

Defamation Act 1996 (c. 31)

33 (1) The Defamation Act 1996 is amended as follows.

(2) In section 17(1) (interpretation), in the definition of "statutory provision", after "1978" there is inserted—

"(aa) a provision contained in an Act of the Scottish Parliament or in an instrument made under such an Act,".

(3) In paragraph 11(1)(c) of Schedule 1 (qualified privilege), after "Minister of the Crown" there is inserted "a member of the Scottish Executive".

Damages Act 1996 (c. 48)

34 In section 6 of the Damages Act 1996 (guarantees for public sector settlements), after subsection (8) there is inserted—

"(8A) In the application of subsection (3) above to Scotland, for the words from "guidelines" to the end there shall be substituted "the Minister"."

SCHEDULE 9

Section 125.

REPEALS

Chapter	*Short title*	*Extent of repeal*
1927 c. 35.	The Sheriff Courts and Legal Officers (Scotland) Act 1927.	In section 1(2), "with the consent of the Treasury".
		In section 2, "with the consent of the Treasury as to numbers and salaries".
		In section 3, "and in either case with the consent of the Treasury".
		In section 5, "with the consent of the Treasury as to numbers and salaries".

Chapter	*Short title*	*Extent of repeal*
		In section 12, "after consultation with the Treasury".
1933 c. 41.	The Administration of Justice (Scotland) Act 1933.	In sections 24(7) and 25, "and shall be exercised on nomination by the Lord Advocate".
1975 c. 24.	The House of Commons Disqualification Act 1975.	In Schedule 2, the entries for the Lord Advocate and the Solicitor General for Scotland.
1975 c. 27.	The Ministerial and other Salaries Act 1975.	In Part III of Schedule 1, the entries for the Lord Advocate and the Solicitor General for Scotland.
1980 c. 44.	The Education (Scotland) Act 1980.	In section 135(1), in the definition of "Her Majesty's inspectors", "on the recommendation of the Secretary of State".
1984 c. 4.	The Tourism (Overseas Promotion) (Scotland) Act 1984.	Section 1(2).
1986 c. 56.	The Parliamentary Constituencies Act 1986.	In Schedule 2, rule 1(2).
1989 c. 45.	The Prisons (Scotland) Act 1989.	Section 2.

Adapted and published by GRANGIS under the OGL Licence 3.0.

www.nationalarchives.gov.uk/doc/open-government-licence/version/3/

GRANGIS - UK PUBLISHING 2022.
Thank you for taking the time to leave us a review regarding this version

★★★★★

For further inquiries, contact us at:
www.grangis.com / contact@grangis.com

www.ingramcontent.com/pod-product-compliance
Lightning Source LLC
LaVergne TN
LVHW060213210926
848481LV00008B/2715